OUTDOOR ESCAPES
Washington, D.C.

Help Us Keep This Guide Up-to-Date

Every effort has been made by the author and editors to make this guide as accurate and useful as possible. However, many things can change after a guide is published—trails are rerouted, regulations change, techniques evolve, facilities come under new management, and so on.

We would love to hear from you concerning your experiences with this guide and how you feel it could be improved and kept up-to-date. While we may not be able to respond to all comments and suggestions, we'll take them to heart and we'll also make certain to share them with the author. Please send your comments and suggestions to the following address:

The Globe Pequot Press
Reader Response/Editorial Department
P.O. Box 480
Guilford, CT 06437

Or you may e-mail us at:

editorial@GlobePequot.com

Thanks for your input, and happy trails!

OUTDOOR ESCAPES
Washington, D.C.

A FOUR-SEASON GUIDE

Kevin J. Carnahan

FALCON®

GUILFORD, CONNECTICUT
HELENA, MONTANA
AN IMPRINT OF THE GLOBE PEQUOT PRESS

Text and page design by Lesley Weissman-Cook
Maps created by Trailhead Graphics © The Globe Pequot Press
Photos on pages 37 and 169 by Jim Shortall. All other photos by Kevin Carnahan.

ISSN 1547–6782
ISBN 0–7627–3056–0

Manufactured in the United States of America
First Edition/First Printing

CAUTION

Outdoor recreation activities are by their very nature potentially hazardous. All participants in such activities must assume the responsibility for their own actions and safety. The information contained in this guidebook cannot replace sound judgment and good decision-making skills, which help reduce risk exposure, nor does the scope of this book allow for disclosure of all the potential hazards and risks involved in such activities.

Learn as much as possible about the outdoor recreation activities you participate in, prepare for the unexpected, and be safe and cautious. The reward will be a safer and more enjoyable experience.

This book is dedicated to my mom.

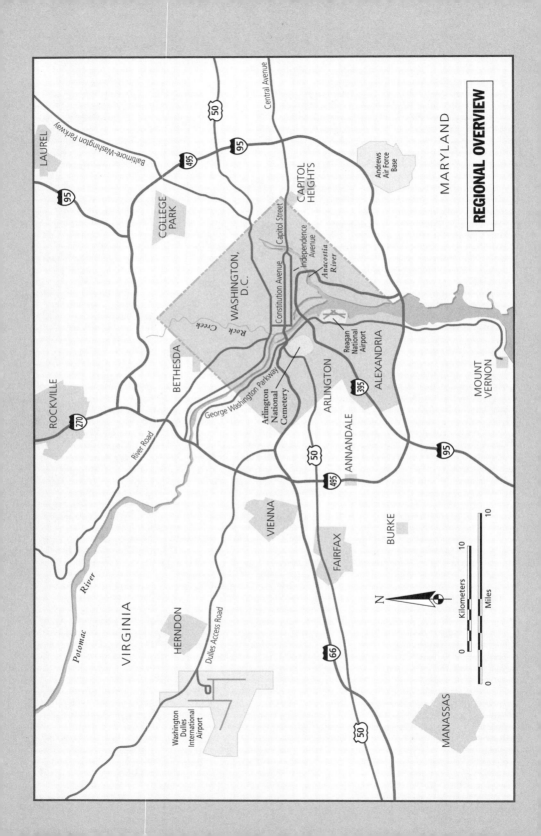

REGIONAL OVERVIEW

CONTENTS

LIST OF MAPS

ACKNOWLEDGMENTS

A very special thank-you to the following people and organizations for their assistance: Ajay Deshpande; all the bird-watchers at Snicker's Gap; Brian Connors; Chris Warner of Earth Treks Climbing; Clarkpoint Croquet Company; Coach Riggs; Connor and Megan Lau; David Lowry of the World Adult Kickball Association; Doug Stroud of East Coast Board Company; Edward M. Nassor; Hope Howard of the Mid-Atlantic Soaring Association; Jim Shortall; Karen Babcock of Ladew Topiary Gardens; Laurie Harris; Marlene Bracamontes; Mary DeAngelus; Melanie Shay; Pat Rea; Patrick M. Reynolds, creator of *Flashbacks;* Pete Ostrom; the Hoppe Family; the Road Runners Club of America; and the U.S. Chess Center.

INTRODUCTION

So you want to find an outdoor adventure, a great new place to visit, or just something fun to do? The Washington, D.C., area has all the resources you need to escape the hustle and bustle of school, work, and some of the worst traffic in the country. Washington is unmatched in scenic beauty, history, and its many opportunities to enjoy nature. Discover a new world right in your own backyard.

To the east lies the mighty Atlantic Ocean. Go surfing at Ocean City, Maryland, or enjoy a stretch of relatively desolate beach along Assateague Island. Wild horses inhabit the island, but they pretty much keep to themselves. A little closer in is the Chesapeake Bay, the largest estuary in the United States and home to millions of oysters, crabs, ducks, geese, and sailboats. You can watch the birds and yachts migrate down the bay.

Bordering us to the west are the Blue Ridge Mountains. It's hard not to be moved by their presence at a distance; it's even better to enjoy them up close and personal.

World-famous cherry blossoms surround the Tidal Basin in spring, setting the scene for great springtime walks.

Sailboats ply the Potomac River in summer, especially during the Governor's Cup Yacht Race.

You can hike quietly on the Appalachian Trail, float silently above on the wind in a sailplane, or climb a rock outcropping overlooking the Shenandoah River. Bird-watching and surfing are found to the east, but this side of the capital has birds of prey and snowboarders.

Between the ocean and mountains are lush green forests, coursing rivers, and open fields—and that's just in the open spaces! For those of you who think we are walled in by the roads and the urban sprawl, think again. Try flying in to D.C. on a clear day. Look down on the farms, suburbs, and city below—you'll see plenty of green, untouched spaces. Washington itself has the Mall, many tiny parks, and Rock Creek Park—one of the largest urban oases in the world. We also enjoy one of the most amazing cityscapes anywhere, and with its low sightline (no building is taller than the Capitol), we can appreciate it rather than being walled in by skyscrapers.

Four distinct seasons showcase our natural resources. Fresh snow in winter blankets the streets and reveals the stark white beauty of the season. Spring has a seemingly endless display of blooms. First come the pear blossoms in the city streets, then the world-famous cherry blossoms hugging the Tidal Basin. Next come the dogwoods of the neighborhoods, followed by azaleas blooming everywhere. Summer is a lush sea of green when the trees fill out. Fall may be the best season of all, with the forests and mountains ablaze in a natural display of fireworks.

Growing up, parents forever told us to "go outside and play." Kids play kickball, pick images out of fluffy clouds, catch fireflies on summer evenings, and go sledding down the steepest hill. As kids become . . . older kids, their games change and become a little more serious. Older kids climb mountains, kayak, run marathons, race bikes, and hang out with their friends at rock concerts. Still older kids are the smartest of all: They like everything the younger kids do and retain an appreciation for the natural world. They walk in the park, bird-watch, take boat tours, play bocce, check out topiary gardens, and ride motorcycles.

Outdoor Escapes is for all kids. Young or old, wild or placid, it doesn't matter. No matter what your physical capacity or your interests, you can find some fun activities, events, and beautiful scenic spots to enjoy here. If you're not sure where to start, open a page at random and see what grabs you.

You don't have to be in top physical condition to have an Outdoor Escape. Within these pages are activities for children, the elderly, the disabled, and the extremely active. Visit a park, take in the theater; there are thousands of outdoor places and activities in the city, and not all of them involve running marathons. Although Washington has that, too.

Here are just a few of the Outdoor Escapes you'll find in and around Washington, D.C.:

- Play kickball on the Mall.
- Learn where you may win a free horse (King or Queen Neptune).
- Take a tour in a World War II amphibious vehicle.
- Watch 19,000 birds of prey fly overhead in one day.
- Listen to a fifty-bell carillon recital while overlooking the monuments of Washington.
- Kayak over a class VI rapid.
- Go see a movie at a drive-in.
- Set up a cricket thermometer with your kids.
- Run in the only major open-registration marathon in the United States, or the largest 5K race in the world.

Fall comes to the Custis Trail in Arlington, Virginia, another great place to experience an outdoor escape.

Great Falls National Park in Virginia and Maryland is beautiful year-round, even in winter.

- Watch the Around the World Yacht Race.
- Visit the best topiary gardens in North America.
- Fly more than 1,000 miles in a glider.
- Watch one of the Triple Crown races.
- Take your bike on the Metro.
- Participate in a Human Chess Match.
- Ski at any of twenty-eight resorts.
- See a free Shakespeare play.
- Ride in Rolling Thunder.
- Learn to play bocce or cricket.
- Climb the only class 7 rock route west of Yosemite.
  And much more!

How to Use This Guide

You may be thinking that every outdoor event, activity, and location in Washington can't possibly be listed in this book—and you're right. As for locations and events, *Outdoor Escapes* is just a starting point. And a good place to begin your explorations might be chapter 1, "Trails." The first chapter is focused on the capital region's best outdoor destinations—places to walk, hike, skate, horseback ride, bicycle, or what have you. Let the trails become your new route of transit.

This book also includes detailed maps of some of the best spots in the metro area. These spots will come up again and again in the chapters that follow, so you can refer back to the maps whenever it's helpful. The maps are located in chapter 1, "Trails." See the "List of Maps" on page xi for a complete listing of maps.

Keep playing through the rest of the chapters. Each one targets a different outdoor sport or activity and then provides safety tips and information for the beginner as well as the expert. You'll find the best places in greater Washington to practice or just play. You'll find chapters on rock climbing, boating (whether a dinner cruise or whitewater kayaking!), stargazing, gliding, even motorcycle riding. Chapter 16, "Snowboarding and Skiing," includes a detailed guide to all twenty-eight of the ski resorts within driving distance of D.C.

Except for some smaller leagues, such as kickball and cricket, the team sports didn't make it into this book. There are so many soccer, lacrosse, flag football, and softball leagues in every corner of the city that it would be impossible to keep track of them all. However, this book tells you where to watch professional sports (that's in chapter 17). Chapter 18, "The Arts," highlights many of D.C.'s best cultural resources—places where you can enrich your mind (through theater, music, literature, and much more) while enjoying the great outdoors. And chapter 19, "Places to Play," is sort of a directory to D.C.'s treasures—listings of monuments and scenic spots where you can stroll and enjoy a moment of solitude and quiet contemplation in this busy world we live in. Chapter 20, "Playdates," is a brief month-by-month listing of the many annual events that can inspire us all to experience and enjoy the outdoors.

Whether you're one of the millions to arrive in Washington in recent years or one of the few, the proud, the natives—take advantage of what's here. Don't treat the outdoor world as we too often do the Smithsonian museums downtown—by visiting only when relatives or friends are in town. Make each day an adventure. Find amazing new places and fun things to do. Go outside and play. Create your own Outdoor Escapes.

1 Trails

IN CENTURIES PAST trails took people from the rural countryside into the towns and marketplaces. Now we use trails to help us escape from the urban life and take us back to nature. Walkers, runners, bikers, people in wheelchairs, in-line skaters, even horses use the many trails that wind through the D.C. metro area. Some folks like the overgrown paths for hiking, others use one of the many paved and graded rail-to-trail paths to get in shape for bike tours in Europe, and still others just want a nice place to stretch their legs. Whatever the reason, go outside and play on the trails.

Trail Safety

No place is perfectly safe 100 percent of the time. Enjoy the day and remember these safety tips so you can have a safer outing.

- *How to act:* Be alert. Be smart. Stay to the right on the trail. Remember that horses and then pedestrians have the right-of-way. Be courteous to all trail users. Obey traffic signals and only cross roads at designated crossings. Look both ways before crossing. Assist others with breakdowns or injuries. Call 911 for emergencies. Trust your intuition about unfamiliar people and areas.
- *What to know:* Check the weather before starting out. Know locations of phone booths or open businesses in the area. Tell friends or family the route you'll be taking and an expected time of return.
- *What to have:* Travel with a partner when possible. Carry an ID, a cell phone or change for a phone call, a whistle, and any emergency medical information necessary. Wear reflective gear. Carry a map, water, and high-energy snacks when traveling long distances.

- **Don'ts:** Don't wear headsets—you need to hear what's going on around you. Don't go to unfamiliar areas when alone.
- **Bikers:** Wear a helmet. Pull off the trail when stopping. Give a warning (voice, bell, or horn) when passing. Keep a maximum distance from others when passing. Don't go faster than 12 miles per hour.
- **In-line skaters:** Wear a helmet, gloves, and kneepads to prevent injury.
- **Horseback riders:** Riders should always wear a safety helmet when riding. When not on a bridle trail, stay on the grass shoulder when possible. On most trails horses have the right-of-way over pedestrians. If you're a pedestrian, get out of the way. Don't approach horses without receiving an okay from their owners.
- **Pet owners:** Clean up after your pet. Keep him on a leash. If your pet is too large for you to control (we've all seen it), take him to training before taking him to the trails. Don't approach pets without receiving an okay from their owners.
- **Motorized vehicles:** Only motorized wheelchairs and service vehicles should be on the trail.

Appalachian Trail

The Appalachian Trail (AT) runs along the crest of the Appalachian Mountains and is one of the most famous—and beautiful—trails in the world. The AT travels 2,160 miles from Springer Mountain, Georgia, to Mount Katahdin, Maine, through fourteen states, eight national forests, and two national parks. There are no fees to hike the AT—it's all on public land.

▶ Potomac Appalachian Trail Club

118 Park Street, SE, Vienna, VA 22180-4609; (703) 242–0693; fax (703) 242–0968; www.patc.net

The Potomac Appalachian Trail Club (PATC) is a volunteer trails organization that maintains and improves nearly 1,000 miles of hiking trails, thirty shelters, and twenty-eight cabins in Virginia, Maryland, West Virginia, Pennsylvania, and the District of Columbia. It has a membership of more than 7,000. No membership is required to join the club on any of its trips; the PATC welcomes newcomers. Its offices are open to the public Monday through Thursday 7:00 to 9:00 P.M., as well as noon to 2:00 P.M. on Thursday and Friday.

D.C. and Maryland Trails

▶ Capital Crescent Trail

Coalition for the Capital Crescent Trail, P. O. Box 30703, Bethesda, MD 20824; (202) 234–4874; www.cctrail.org

The Capital Crescent Trail runs from Georgetown through Bethesda to Silver Spring. The 12-mile trail was once the old Georgetown Branch of the B&O Railroad. Like most rail-to-trail projects, it features gentle gradients—fun for walkers, runners, bikers, in-line skaters, and even cross-country skiers when we've got enough snow. Try it for a day out—it's only 5 miles from downtown Bethesda to Fletcher's Boat House, and from there another 2 miles to the Georgetown waterfront. Most of the trail is through parks or other wooded areas.

The Coalition for the Capital Crescent Trail has lead the way in creating the trail as well as ensuring its safety, beauty, and fun. Contact this group for membership information or for a Capital Crescent Trail Map.

▶ Anacostia Tributary Trail System

Northern Prince George's County, MD; (301) 699–2407; TTY (301) 699–2544; www.pgparks.com

This large Y-shaped path runs for 20 miles along the tributaries of the Anacostia River. Compared to other trails, this one isn't in the best shape, but you get a beautiful barrier-free greenway without the huge crowds often found elsewhere. The southernmost point of the trail is located at Colmar Manor Community Park. Open sunrise to sunset.

▶ U.S. National Arboretum

24th and R Streets, NE, Washington, DC; (202) 245–2726; www.usna.usda.gov

An amazing forested park with 446 acres and 9.5 miles of winding roadways, the U.S. National Arboretum is the only federally funded arboretum in the country—supported by both public tax dollars and private contributions.

Ponds and streams lace the park, while nature trails wind among foreign and domestic trees. Or you can experience the National Arboretum via tram. An open-air tram tour only takes about forty minutes and is an easy, fun way to see all the plant collections and gardens. Tram tours are available on weekends only, and tickets must be purchased on the day of your tour; call the arboretum for times and prices.

The arboretum is open 8:00 A.M. to 5:00 P.M. daily. There's no admission fee.

▶ National Zoological Park ("the Zoo")

3001 Connecticut Avenue, NW, Washington, DC; (202) 673–4800; natzoo.si.edu

Lions and tigers and bears—*oh my!* The Zoo is known for animals, not trails . . . but it has trails in abundance. You can't ride a bike or skate through it, but if you're looking for a place to go walking or for an early-morning run (before all the buildings open), the Zoo really is a great place to go. It's also now the home of two pandas, Mei Xiang and Tian Tian, as well as a baby elephant, Kandula.

From May through September 15, the zoo grounds are open daily 6:00 A.M. to 8:00 P.M. From September 16 through April, they're open until 6:00 P.M. Closed December 25. See chapter 19, "Places to Play," for more information.

▶ National Mall

Between Constitution and Independence Avenues, SW, Washington, DC; www.nps.gov/nama

While it's not exactly a trail, many people go running, walking, or in-line skating down on the Mall. The grassy strip is lined with 2,000 American elms to add shade in summer and color in fall. It extends approximately 2 miles from the U.S. Capitol to the Lincoln Memorial. Enjoy spectacular views of the monuments and Smithsonian buildings. Open daily.

▶ Fort Dupont Park

Randle Circle, SE, Washington, DC; (202) 426–7723; www.nps.gov/fodu

A heavily wooded park with numerous trails running through its 376 acres, Fort Dupont was built in 1861 to guard against Confederate attacks. Rangers lead nature walks from the park's activity center. The park is open daily from dawn until dusk; the activity center's hours are Monday through Friday 7:45 A.M. to 4:15 P.M.

▶ Rock Creek Park

Rock Creek Nature Center, 5200 Glover Road, NW, Washington, DC; (202) 895–6070; www.nps.gov/rocr

Trails follow Rock Creek from Georgetown to the Maryland state line (near Bethesda) in this 1,754-acre national park. Its beautiful valley setting is very different from the rest of Washington's terrain. Created in 1890 and one of the largest urban parks in the country, Rock Creek is only 5 miles from the White House. It's a step away from the bustle of the crowded city and enjoyed by runners, walkers, bikers, skaters, and birders.

The park is open during daylight hours. Dogs are allowed in Rock Creek Park as long as they're on a leash. If you want to ride your horse, you may park your trailer at the nature center, but you must stick to the designated bridle trails. Nature walks are offered from the nature center on Sunday at 2:00 P.M. year-round.

▶ Chesapeake & Ohio (C&O) Canal Towpath

30th and Jefferson Streets, NW, Washington, DC; (202) 653–5190

The towpath is popular for walking, running, birding, biking, horseback riding, and cross-country skiing; it's wheelchair accessible. It's not the easiest surface to travel on a road bike with thin tires, but is fine for cruisers, hybrids, and mountain bikes (bigger tires make it easier with the rough surface). Most of the traffic on the trail is between Great Falls, Maryland, and Georgetown—farther out is less congested. No matter where you go, however, you'll see many old locks, lock houses, and other old structures that take you back to the days of the canal's original use. Open daily, dawn to dusk.

The C&O Canal Association (www.cando canal.org) was created to protect, preserve, and promote the assets of the C&O Canal Historic Park. The group also sponsors hikes and bike trips.

The Allegheny Trail Alliance (www.atatrail. org) has first-rate maps along with locations of places to eat and sleep along the trail for people on long hikes.

RAILS-TO-TRAILS CONSERVANCY

The Rail-to-Trails Conservancy helps create rail-trails (multiuse paths) from abandoned railroad corridors. Public ownership is maintained in case rail service is needed at a later date. Several of the major railroads support Rails-to-Trails Conservancy activities. The trails have gentle grades and are ideal for recreational use. If you'd like to help build and manage trails, contact the conservancy for membership information at Rails-to-Trails National Headquarters, 1100 17th Street, NW; Washington, DC 20036; (202) 331–9696; www.railtrails.org. It also has lots of news about trails all over the country.

▶ Baltimore and Annapolis Trail

East Coast Greenway, www.greenway.org; B&A Trail Ranger Station, (410) 222–6244

The B&A Trail was created on the former Washington, Baltimore & Annapolis (WB&A) rail line and is now part of the East Coast Greenway. This rail-trail starts just north of Annapolis at the Jonas Green Park and runs 15.5 miles northwest through Severna Park to Glen Burnie at Dorsey Road. The trail runs very close to Baltimore Washington International Airport (BWI), where it connects up with the BWI Trail. The paved B&A Trail runs parallel to the Severna River and is excellent for running, walking, cross-country skiing, biking, and in-line skating.

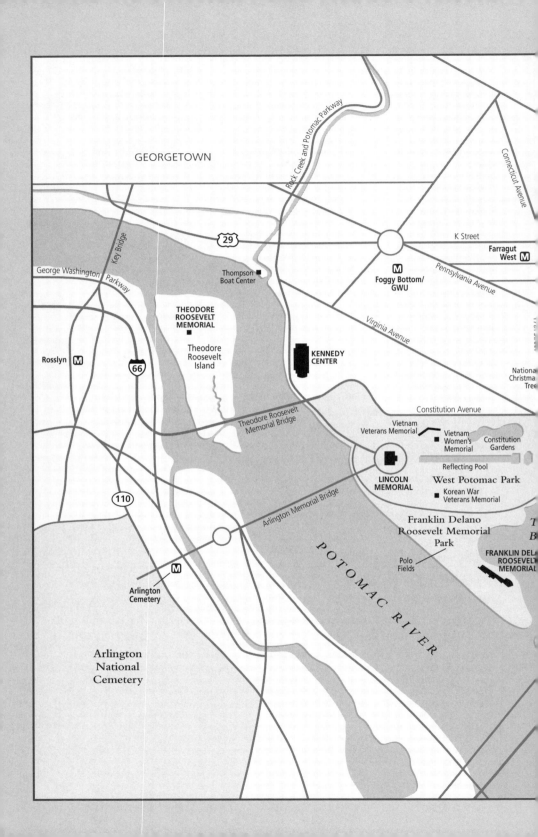

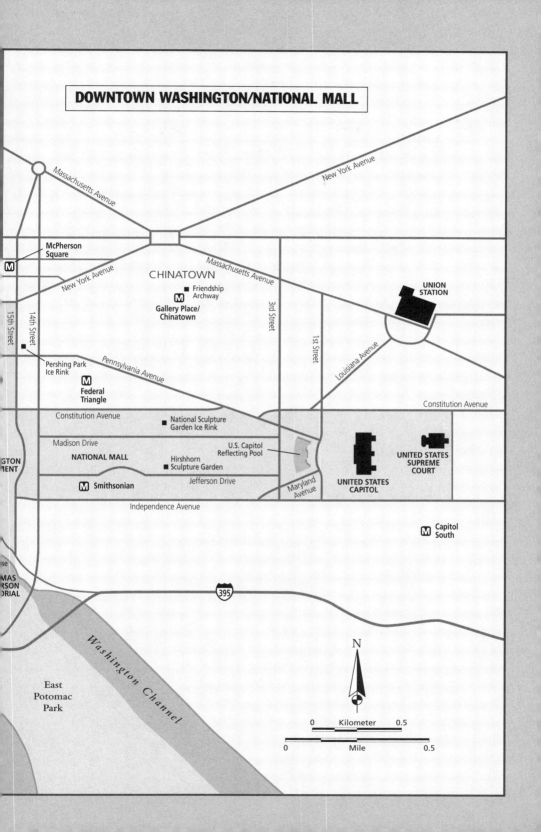

DOWNTOWN WASHINGTON/NATIONAL MALL

Massachusetts Avenue

New York Avenue

McPherson
Square

Ⓜ

New York Avenue

CHINATOWN

Massachusetts Avenue

■ Friendship
Archway
Ⓜ
Gallery Place/
Chinatown

3rd Street

1st Street

Louisiana Avenue

UNION
STATION

15th Street

14th Street

Pershing Park
Ice Rink
Ⓜ
Federal
Triangle

Pennsylvania Avenue

Constitution Avenue

Constitution Avenue

Madison Drive

NATIONAL MALL

■ National Sculpture
Garden Ice Rink

U.S. Capitol
Reflecting Pool

Hirshhorn
■ Sculpture Garden

Ⓜ Smithsonian

Jefferson Drive

Maryland
Avenue

UNITED STATES
CAPITOL

UNITED STATES
SUPREME
COURT

Independence Avenue

Ⓜ Capitol
South

GTON
ENT

se

MAS
RSON
ORIAL

395

N

East
Potomac
Park

Washington Channel

0   Kilometer   0.5

0   Mile   0.5

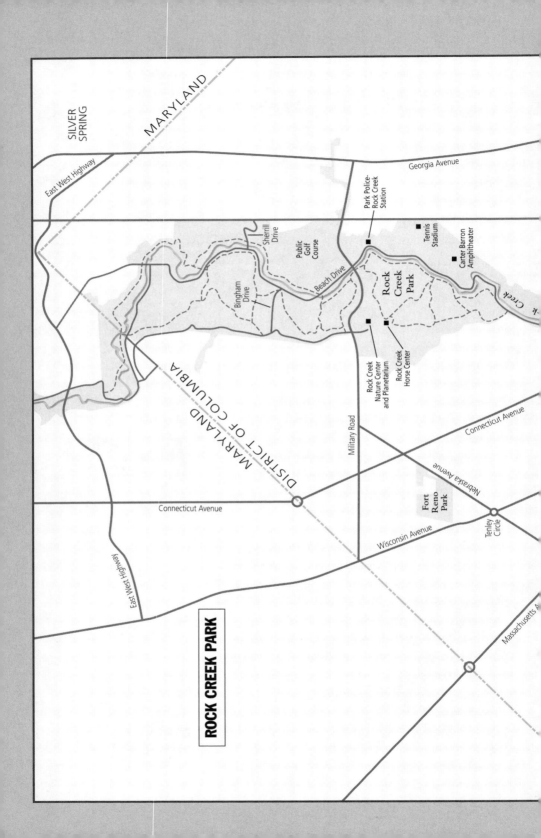

ROCK CREEK PARK

SILVER SPRING

MARYLAND

East West Highway

Georgia Avenue

Sherrill Drive

Park Police-
Rock Creek
Station

Public
Golf
Course

Tennis
Stadium

Carter Barron
Amphitheater

Bingham
Drive

Beach Drive

Rock
Creek
Park

Creek

Rock Creek
Nature Center
and Planetarium

Rock Creek
Horse Center

Military Road

MARYLAND

DISTRICT OF COLUMBIA

Connecticut Avenue

Nebraska Avenue

Connecticut Avenue

Fort
Reno
Park

Tenley
Circle

Wisconsin Avenue

East West Highway

Massachusetts A

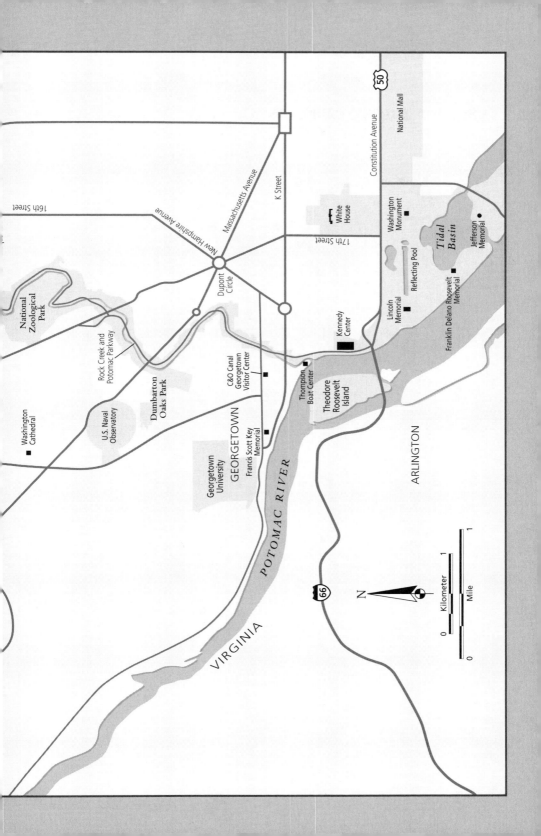

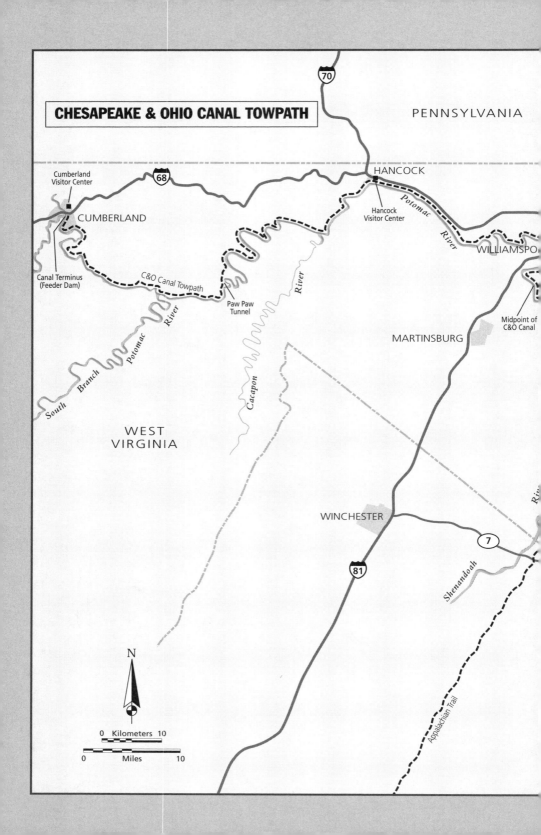

CHESAPEAKE & OHIO CANAL TOWPATH

PENNSYLVANIA

70

68

Cumberland
Visitor Center

HANCOCK

CUMBERLAND

Potomac

Hancock
Visitor Center

River

WILLIAMSPO

Canal Terminus
(Feeder Dam)

C&O Canal Towpath

River

Midpoint of
C&O Canal

Paw Paw
Tunnel

River

Potomac

MARTINSBURG

River

Cacapon

Branch

South

WEST
VIRGINIA

WINCHESTER

Riv

7

81

N

Shenandoah

Appalachian Trail

0   Kilometers 10

0   Miles   10

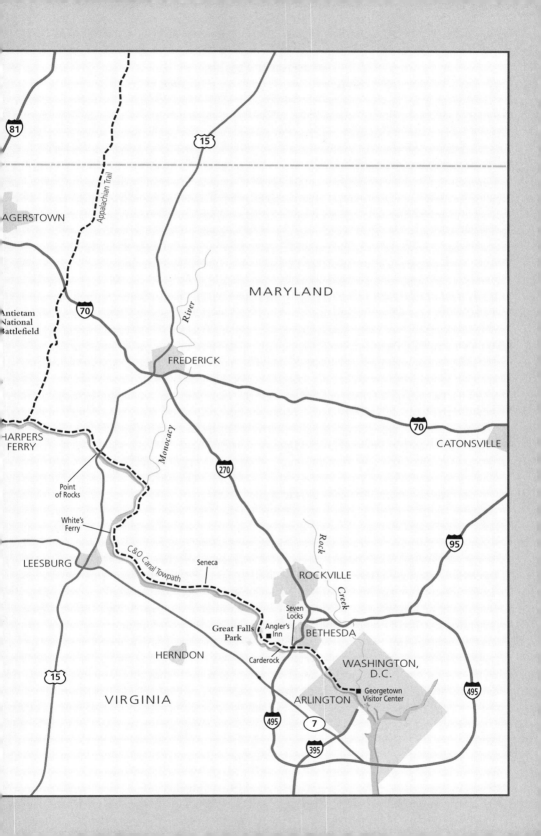

Virginia Trails

▶ Theodore Roosevelt Island

(703) 289–2550; www.nps.gov/gwmp/tri.htm

Theodore Roosevelt Island sits in the middle of the Potomac between Rosslyn, Virginia, and Georgetown. The ninety-one-acre wooded island makes a fitting memorial to the conservationist president who once said, "The nation behaves well if it treats the natural resources as assets which it must turn over to the next generation increased and not impaired in value." The outdoor memorial includes a statue and thought-provoking quotes—appropriately placed in this escape from urban life.

Many nature trails lead through the marsh, swamp, and forest. The swamp is on the back side of the island (the Georgetown side) and may have a few too many mosquitoes for some during summer months. The island habitat includes an interesting collection of birds and small animals. Often, bird-watchers and runners use the trail that loops around the perimeter of the island, and you'll find an up-close and unobstructed view of the Georgetown waterfront from the back side.

The TRI parking lot is the starting location for many different trails. You can take the Mount Vernon Trail to the south, the Potomac Heritage Trail to the north, the Custis Trail through Arlington to meet up with the W&OD Trail, or cross the Key Bridge and jump on the C&O Canal Towpath. (Look for descriptions of all these trails elsewhere in this chapter.) No bikes are allowed on the island; dogs must be kept on a leash. The parking lot (which fills up early on weekends) is accessible by car only from the GW Parkway northbound (before the Key Bridge). A pedestrian bridge over the parkway is accessible from Rosslyn, Virginia, near the Key Bridge.

▶ Potomac Heritage National Scenic Trail

www.nps.gov

One of the most scenic hiking venues in the area, the Potomac Heritage Trail parallels the George Washington Memorial Parkway along the Potomac River. The 10-mile trail runs from the north end of the Theodore Roosevelt Island parking lot (near Rosslyn, Virginia, and across the Key Bridge from Georgetown; see above) north to the Beltway at the American Legion Bridge. The path is maintained by members of the Potomac Appalachian Trail Club and can be difficult or even dangerous to travel in wet weather. Blue markers show the trail route; yellow markers show the routes out to various access points.

These access points include Live Oak Drive (north of the Cabin John Bridge), Turkey Run Park (at trail mile 8.3; parking available), Fort Marcy (mile 4.9; again, there's parking here), North Glebe Road at Route 123, Gulf Branch (the intersection of 36th and Nelson Streets), Donaldson Run (at the parking lots near the end of Marcy Street in Potomac Overlook Park), Windy Run (end of Kenmore Street), and Theodore Roosevelt Island.

There are steep, rocky hillsides, and many of the streams are crossed by stepping on the rocks. Be careful of high water, slippery rocks, or ice in winter. Nevertheless, this is truly a beautiful forested trail with some amazing views of the Potomac. You'll come across some interesting sites that you never thought you'd find inside the Beltway, including the waterfall at Dead Run. This is a natural trail, not a paved walkway weaving through the forest. Take care to wear appropriate clothing and footwear.

▶ Mount Vernon Trail

National Park Service, George Washington Memorial Parkway, Turkey Run Park, McLean, VA 22101; (703) 285–2600; www.nps.gov

Easily the most scenic trail in the D.C. area, the Mount Vernon Trail parallels the George Washington Memorial Parkway along the Potomac River. The 18.5-mile trail runs from the south end of the Theodore Roosevelt Island parking lot (near Rosslyn, Virginia, and across the Key Bridge from Georgetown) south to George Washington's plantation located at Mount Vernon (see chapter 19, "Places to Play").

The trail offers amazing views of the monuments in Washington, running past, among other highlights:

- Arlington National Cemetery.
- Memorial Bridge.
- Lady Bird Park.
- The Pentagon.
- Navy and Marine Memorial.
- Gravelly Point (north end of the airport, where you can watch the planes take off).
- Ronald Reagan Washington National Airport.
- Daingerfield Island and the Washington Sailing Marina.
- Old Town Alexandria.
- Jones Point Lighthouse.
- Belle Haven Park/Marina.
- Dyke Marsh Preserve.
- Fort Hunt Park.
- Riverside Park.
- And, of course, our first president's estate and gardens.

One word of caution: Be careful when traveling around Old Town, because there are two routes through town. If you're traveling south, try taking the unmarked trail to the left after the Washington Sailing Marina. It will take you down closer to Potomac and Union Streets.

The paved pathway is used by walkers, runners, bikers, and skaters.

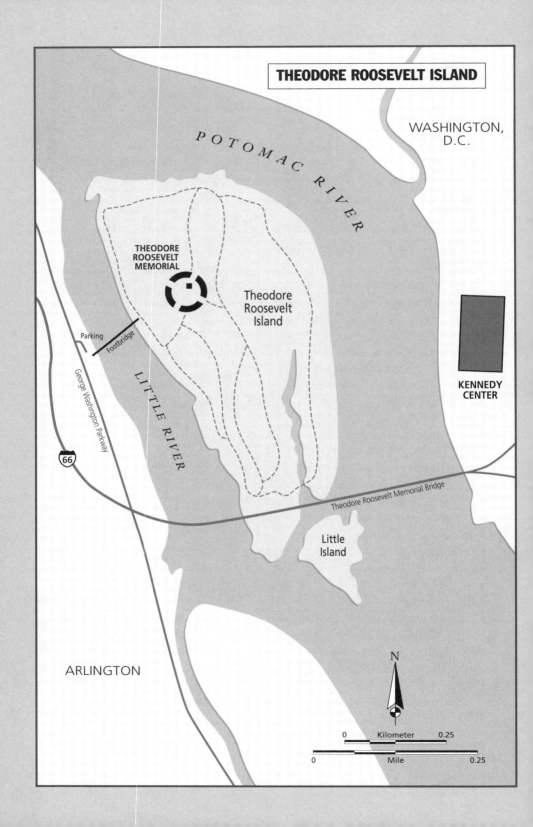

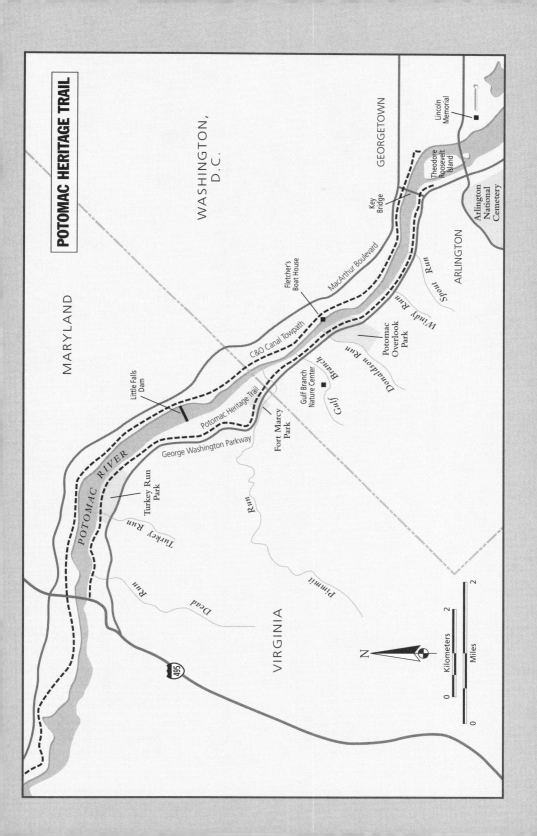

POTOMAC HERITAGE TRAIL

MARYLAND

WASHINGTON, D.C.

GEORGETOWN

Lincoln Memorial

Theodore Roosevelt Island

Key Bridge

Arlington National Cemetery

ARLINGTON

Spout Run

Fletcher's Boat House

MacArthur Boulevard

Windy Run

Potomac Overlook Park

Donaldson Run

C&O Canal Towpath

Gulf Branch Nature Center

Gulf Branch

Little Falls Dam

Potomac Heritage Trail

Fort Marcy Park

George Washington Parkway

POTOMAC RIVER

Turkey Run Park

Turkey Run

Run

Pimmit Run

Dead Run

VIRGINIA

495

N

Kilometers

0   2

Miles

0   2

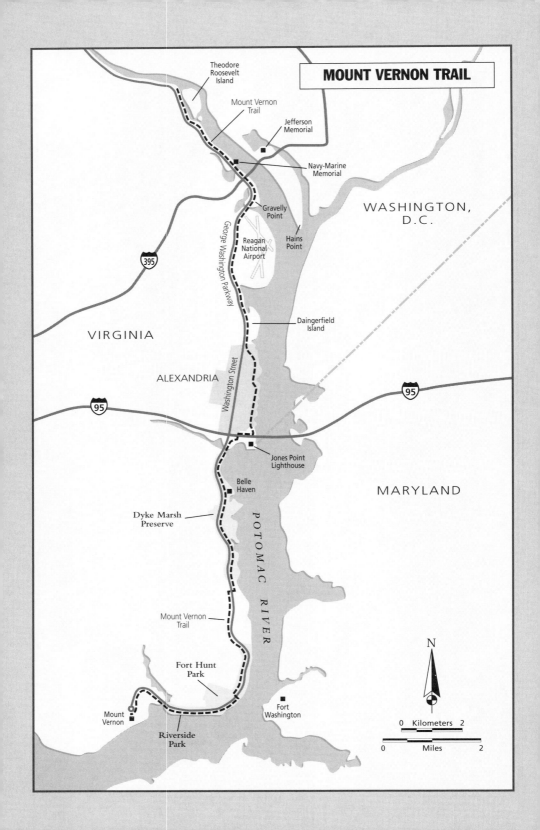

MOUNT VERNON TRAIL

Theodore
Roosevelt
Island

Mount Vernon
Trail

Jefferson
Memorial

Navy-Marine
Memorial

Gravelly
Point

Hains
Point

WASHINGTON,
D.C.

George Washington Parkway

Reagan
National
Airport

395

VIRGINIA

Daingerfield
Island

ALEXANDRIA

Washington Street

95

95

Jones Point
Lighthouse

Belle
Haven

MARYLAND

Dyke Marsh
Preserve

POTOMAC RIVER

Mount Vernon
Trail

Fort Hunt
Park

Fort
Washington

N

Mount
Vernon

Riverside
Park

0   Kilometers   2

0   Miles   2

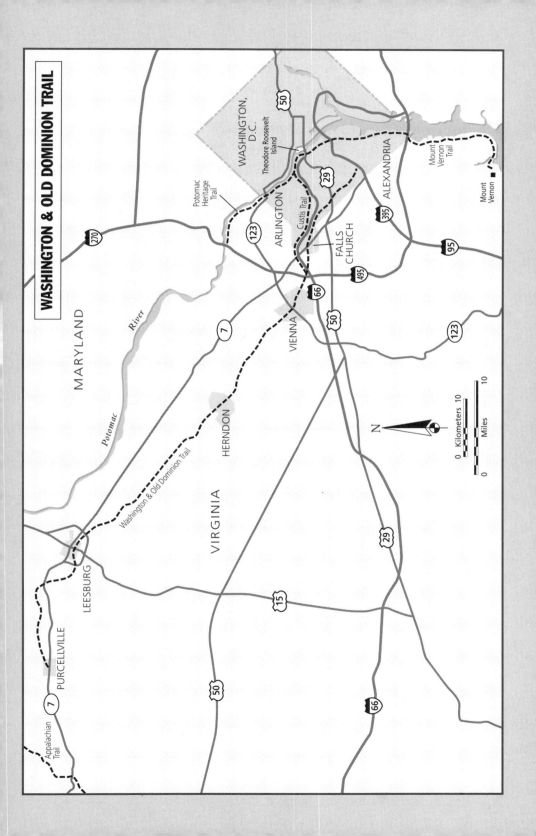

WASHINGTON & OLD DOMINION TRAIL

MARYLAND

Potomac River

VIRGINIA

WASHINGTON, D.C.

Theodore Roosevelt Island

Potomac Heritage Trail

Custis Trail

ARLINGTON

FALLS CHURCH

ALEXANDRIA

Mount Vernon Trail

Mount Vernon

VIENNA

HERNDON

Washington & Old Dominion Trail

LEESBURG

PURCELLVILLE

Appalachian Trail

270

50

29

123

395

495

66

7

50

15

29

50

66

123

95

N

0 Kilometers 10
0 Miles 10

▶ Washington & Old Dominion Trail (W&OD)

Washington & Old Dominion Railroad Regional Park, right off Route 28 at Steeplechase Drive

Northern Virginia Regional Park Authority (NVRPA), 21293 Smiths Switch Road, Ashburn, VA 20147-6016; (703) 729–0596; www.nvrpa.org

Friends of the W&OD Trail, 21293 Smiths Switch Road, Ashburn, VA 20147-6016; (703) 729–0596; www.wodfriends.org

The W&OD Trail runs from Shirlington near I–395 in Arlington County all the way out to Purcellville in Loudoun County at the foot of the Blue Ridge Mountains. On top of the ridge is the Appalachian Trail, but there is currently no connection between the two.

Another rail-trail, the former Washington & Old Dominion Railroad is now a 45-mile paved footway used for running, walking, biking, skating, cross-country skiing, bird-watching, or simply for nature strolls. There are 30 miles of adjacent gravel bridle trails for horseback riding. The trail runs through and is accessible in Arlington, Falls Church, Vienna, Reston, Herndon, Sterling, Ashburn, and Leesburg. It's open all year from dawn to dusk. The fifty-four-page color *W&OD Trail Guide* is for sale at all regional parks and at NVRPA headquarters.

▶ The Custis Trail (Arlington)

While the W&OD is a great trail, it doesn't quite get you to downtown D.C. The Custis Trail intersects the W&OD Trail (see above) at mile 4 and parallels I–66 through Arlington. You can either take the 4-mile-long paved trail down to the Key Bridge and cross over to Georgetown, or take the walkway over the GW Parkway to the Theodore Roosevelt Island parking lot. From the parking lot you can cross the bridge to the island and enjoy the nature paths, take the Mount Vernon Trail south to George's plantation, or head north up the Potomac Heritage Trail to the American Legion Bridge. (See the full trail descriptions elsewhere in this chapter.)

▶ Bluemont Junction Trail (Arlington)

Arlington County Bicycle Coordinator, 2100 Clarendon Boulevard, Suite 717, Arlington, VA 23336; (703) 228–3699; www.co.arlington.va.us/dpw/planning/bike.htm

This short asphalt Arlington County path runs 1.3 miles from the W&OD Trail in Bluemont Park to Fairfax Drive in Ballston. As Ballston gets larger, more people are using this trail for commuting in addition to recreational uses. There is a difficult and somewhat dangerous crossing at the intersection of Wilson Boulevard and George Mason Drive; please be careful.

The Custis Trail in Arlington intersects the W&OD Trail.

▶ Accotink Trail

Lake Accotink Park, Fairfax Park Authority, 3701 Pender Drive, Fairfax, VA 22030; (703) 569–0285; www.fairfaxcounty.gov/parks/accotink

The gravel-and-asphalt Accotink Trail is 3.75 miles long. Several other local trails run into it, so don't think you can only get there from the park entrance. It's great for biking, hiking, and bird-watching because you go around the lake. In addition to the great blue heron, don't be surprised if you see some fly anglers here as well: The streams have been stocked with trout in the recent years.

▶ Colvin Run Stream Valley Horse Trail

This trail begins one block off the W&OD Trail (near mile 17; see W&OD earlier in this chapter) on Michael Farraday Court. The 3-mile natural-surface path runs through the wooded valley of Colvin Run Stream Valley through Lake Fairfax Park, across Hunter Mill Road, and ends at Route 7 across from Colvin Mill.

The Eastern Shore

▶ Assateague Island

Assateague Island National Seashore, National Park Service, 8586 Beach Road, Chincoteague, VA 23336; (410) 641–1441 or (757) 336–6577; www.nps.gov/asis

Assateague State Park, 7307 Stephen Decatur Highway, Berlin, MD 21811; (410) 641–2120; reservations (888) 432–CAMP (2267); www.dnr.state.md.us/publiclands/eastern/assateague.html

The uncrowded beaches of this Maryland/Virginia island are windswept, pristine, and wonderful for nature-watching. The 0.5-mile Dunes Trail lies just beyond a traffic circle at the southern tip of Bayberry Drive. Assateague Island on the Delmarva Peninsula is home to the famed Chincoteague ponies and has about 15 miles of trails; the ponies can often be seen from the roads and trails. A seven-day car pass for Assateague Island (both the national seashore and the refuge) is available at the gate for approximately $5.00. There's no fee for bikers or hikers. Parking lots are available next to the beach and near most of the trails on the refuge. No pets allowed.

▶ Chincoteague National Wildlife Refuge

Refuge Manager, Chincoteague National Wildlife Refuge, Chincoteague, VA 23336; (757) 336–6122; chinco.fws.gov

The Virginia portion of Assateague Island has biking and hiking trails, beaches, marshes, and waterfowl. The refuge is open daily 5:00 A.M. to 10:00 P.M.; the visitor center, daily 9:00 A.M. to 4:00 P.M. The entrance fee (about $4.00) is good for seven days.

Seasonal Walking Opportunities

▶ The Cherry Blossoms of Washington

Cherry blossoms signify the end of winter for Washingtonians. We crawl out of our winter shells and migrate down to the Tidal Basin after watching the news to see which weekend will be the "peak" time. Walking the Tidal Basin has become the springtime event for Washingtonians.

The 1,300 cherry trees enclose the Tidal Basin and wrap themselves down around Hains Point. There are also several groves around the Washington Monument.

The history of the blossoms goes back to 1910, when the mayor of Tokyo, Yukio Ozaki, sent a gift of 2,000 trees to the city of Washington. Unfortunately, the trees that arrived were infested with insects and disease and had to be burned. Healthy trees were then specially selected from along the Arakawa River and, in 1912, 3,000 of them arrived in Washington. The first were planted by First Lady Taft and Viscountess Chinda, the Japanese ambassador's wife.

The bloom times depend on how long our Washington winter lasts. The earliest blooming on record occurred on March 20; the latest, on April 20. The average is April 5. The Smithsonian Metro stop gets overcrowded with tourists during the peak times, so you might want to try another stop close by. When the Tidal Basin is packed, check out Hains Point. The trees are just as beautiful, and the crowds are almost nonexistent. For up-to-date information on the peak bloom, check out the National Park Service Web site at www.nps.gov/cherry/.

▶ Ladew Topiary Gardens

3535 Jarrettsville Pike, Monkton, MD 21111; (410) 557–9570; www.ladewgardens.com

Yes, Ladew is north of Baltimore and an hour and a half away—but if you have the chance to visit this attraction, you'll understand why it's a must-see. The best topiary garden in the country was started by a self-taught gardener, Harvey S. Ladew. There are fifteen thematic "garden rooms." Garden tours (1.5 miles of trails) are self-guiding around the twenty-two acres. There is also an annual plant sale, and the My Lady's Manor Steeplechase is held in spring for the benefit of the gardens (see chapter 7, "Equestrian Activitites"). There's a cafe, too. Open from mid-April through October, Monday through Friday 10:00 A.M. to 4:00 P.M., Saturday and Sunday 10:30 A.M. to 5:00 P.M.

To get there: Take the Baltimore Beltway (I–695) toward Towson to exit 27B (north). Go north on Route 146 (Dulaney Valley Road). After the Loch Raven

Reservoir Bridge, bear left onto Jarrettsville Pike (Route 146). Ladew Gardens is located on your right, 5 miles north of the stoplight in Jacksonville.

▶ The Maize Maze at Temple Hill Regional Park

Temple Hall Lane, Leesburg, VA; MAIZE information (703) 777–6732; field-trip reservations (703) 779–9372; www.nvrpa.org/maize.html

Corn mazes are an interesting combination of hike and puzzle. More and more are popping up around the area as distressed farmers realize they can make more money in admissions than they can on the corn. Go out and support the farmers and have some fun exploring the maze. Not just for kids, many maize mazes are open late—you have to navigate with the help of a lantern. Many mazes incorporate other farm elements, such as farmers' markets, hayrides, and pick-your-own pumpkins. People are around to help you if you get lost. Open from the end of August through October.

For mazes around the country, check out www.cornfieldmaze.com.

2 Walking

WASHINGTON AND ITS SURROUNDING AREAS were made for walking. Short blocks, easy layouts, and beautiful surroundings make downtown, the Mall, Georgetown, Arlington, Old Town Alexandria, and Bethesda great places to go walking. Stroll the Mall and enjoy the 2,000 American elms that add shade in summer and color in fall. Walk the monuments and museums—from the Vietnam Memorial to the Natural History Museum, the Sculpture Garden, and the Museum of American Art. You may love the peace of Arlington National Cemetery or the National Arboretum. Or maybe you'd prefer the gardens of Georgetown in spring. Even the president traditionally walks part of the inauguration parade.

Walking is one of the best ways to get into shape and stay in shape. It's a good way to build up to running, or can be fun all by itself. Its many health benefits include lowering your cholesterol, blood pressure, and risk of heart attack; increasing your mobility; and helping minimize bone loss—and it's low impact as well. A 2-mile walk three or four times a week at a fast pace will help you lose weight—in fact, walking burns more calories than running over an equal distance.

Walking can be a solitary event, or you can go out with a friend. While most people walk in

GETTING STARTED

- Find a shoe that fits—one that doesn't bind at the toes or across the top of the foot. Your heel shouldn't slip, and the shoe should be flexible at the ball of your foot. Most running stores have shoes specifically for walking as well.
- Wear cotton socks.
- Stretch before and after you walk.
- Start a regular walking routine and gradually increase your distance.
- As always, consult with your physician before starting any physical fitness program.

Walkers enjoy strolling along the banks of the C&O Canal.

their own neighborhoods, it might be fun to try one of the many trails in the Washington, D.C., area—most are fairly flat and ideal for people starting out. Many walkers enjoy the many area shopping malls as well: They're large, usually very safe, and you don't have to worry about bad weather.

Walking Tours

D.C. is famous for all its sites—and there may be no better way to see them than on foot. Get up close and see the way people used to get around the city. If you've toured the city before, try it from this different viewpoint.

▶ D.C. Walking Tours

2844 Wisconsin Avenue, NW, Suite 310, Washington, DC 20007; (202) 237–7534; www.dcwalkingtours.com

Old Town Alexandria Visitor Center, 221 King Street, Alexandria, VA 22314; (800) 388–9119 or (703) 548–0100

There are many ghost walks in the area, and one of the best is in Old Town Alexandria. Take a lantern tour of Old Town, and get a history of the town and the ghosts that inhabit it. Not recommended for small children. Weather permitting, tours depart from the visitor center April through September, Friday and Saturday at 9:00 P.M. The October tour schedule is significantly expanded so we can all enjoy those things that go bump in the night.

▶ Ghost Walk to the Grave of Edgar Allan Poe

Westminster Hall and Burying Ground, Fayette and Green Streets, Baltimore, MD; (410) 706–7228; www.eapoe.org

RACE WALKING

Most running races also offer combined walk competitions, but race walking is different. There is a grace to this sport unlike many others. Trying to go as fast as you can while having one foot on the ground at all times is easier said than done. Don't knock it till ya try it. For more information contact the American Walking Association, USA Track & Field, P. O. Box 120, Indianapolis, IN 46206; (317) 261–0500; www.usatf.org. This is the sanctioning body for race walking.

Yes, the ultimate ghost walk is this visit to Edgar Allan Poe's grave, a stone's throw away in Baltimore. The Halloween Tour includes readings from Edgar Allan Poe's works, other activities, and a visit to Poe's grave. The small fee charged benefits the Westminster Preservation Trust. How did Poe really die? The old romanticized theory was that he drank himself to death. Newer medical diagnosis indicates he may have died of rabies. Either way, not a pretty death for the author who taught us what terror was all about.

WalkAmerica

WalkAmerica is the March of Dimes's biggest fund-raiser. Since 1970 these walkathons have raised more than $1 billion to help give babies a fighting chance. Funds support lifesaving research and innovative programs that prevent prematurity, birth defects, and other infant health problems.

WalkAmerica takes place in all fifty states, the District of Columbia, and Puerto Rico. Most of the walks are held at the end of April or the beginning of May. More than nine million men, women, and children will participate as sponsors, volunteers, and walkers this year! Maybe you can be one of them. For information on the event as a whole, visit www.walkamerica.org or www.marchofdimes.com. See the next page for a list of local walks.

WALKAMERICA WALKATHONS

LOCATION	WALKATHON SITE	DIVISION	PHONE
Washington, D.C.	Washington, D.C.	District Division	(703) 824–0111
Virginia	Springfield, Lake Accotink Park	Northern Virginia Division	(703) 824–0111
	Fairfax Reston, Lake Fairfax Park	Northern Virginia Division	(703) 824–0111
	Loudoun (Leesburg)	Northern Virginia Division	(703) 824–0111
	Fauquier (Warrenton)	Airlie Center, Northern Virginia Division	(703) 824–0111
	Fredericksburg, Old Mill Park	Central Virginia Division	(804) 968–4120
	Culpeper, Yowell Meadow Park	Shenandoah Valley Division	(540) 434–7789
	Front Royal, Bing Crosby Stadium	Shenandoah Valley Division	(540) 434–7789
	Winchester, Winchester Medical Center	Shenandoah Valley Division	(540) 434–7789
Maryland	Prince George's County, Watkins Park—Upper Marlboro	Suburban Maryland Division	(410) 752–7990
	Howard County/ Columbia	Central Maryland Division	(410) 752–7990
	Southern Maryland/ La Plata	Suburban Maryland Division	(410) 752–7990
	Anne Arundel/Annapolis, Navy Marine Corps Stadium	Central Maryland Division	(410) 752–7990
	Montgomery County/ Rockville	Central Maryland Division	(410) 752–7990
	Baltimore City, Legg Mason Plaza	Central Maryland Division	(410) 752–7990
	Frederick, Baker Park	Western Maryland Division	(301) 722–5818
	Baltimore County/ White Marsh	Central Maryland Division	(410) 752–7990
	Harford/Forest Hill	Central Maryland Division	(410) 752–7990

3 Running

RUNNING IS A GREAT WAY to get into shape and stay in shape, whether you head out on your own or join a running club. Many people run in their own neighborhoods, but you might like to try one of the many trails in the Washington, D.C., area—most are fairly flat and ideal for people starting out.

Shoes

Not much is needed in the way of running equipment except the shoes. Comfortable clothes that breathe are important. But the importance of good shoes for running or walking can't be stressed enough. If you plan to spend a number of hours running around, why not spend a little time picking out the proper footwear? There are several high-quality running stores in the area that can help you pick out the proper shoes for you.

I spent about an hour one day picking out my running shoes at Fleet Feet. The folks there not only helped me into a shoe that properly fit my foot, but also watched my running to determine my stride and how I land on my foot—all factors that affect the best shoe for running or walking. And I couldn't tell the difference in price from any of the larger superstores around.

The superstores may have a larger number of shoes, but most are lacking when it comes to variety of sizes—especially in width. And few can offer expert staff who can help you with shoe selection. Remember—you don't buy running shoes based on the color or how they look; you buy them because they fit your feet properly!

▶ Pacers

1301 King Street, Old Town Alexandria, VA 22314; (703) 836–1463;
www.runpacers.com

Pacers is an excellent running store with apparel, shoes, accessories, and coaching.

▶ Fleet Feet Sports

There are a number of Fleet Feet in the area:

7516 Leesburg Pike, Falls Church, VA 22043-2005; (703) 790–3338

6119 B Backlick Road, Springfield, VA 22150, (703) 913–0313

1841 Columbia Road, NW, Washington, DC 20009; (202) 387–3888

Running Safety

Outdoor Escapes suggests you always be aware of your surroundings, wear reflective material, obey the traffic rules, and carry a noisemaker. Run in familiar areas, or with a companion; or be sure someone knows your route and expected time of return. For a complete set of running safety tips, contact the Road Runners Club of America.

▶ Road Runners Club of America (RRCA)

510 North Washington Street, Alexandria, VA 22314; (703) 836–0558;
fax (703) 836–4430; www.rrca.org; office@rrca.org

The Road Runners Club of America is a national organization of 700 not-for-profit running clubs and 200,000 members dedicated to promoting long-distance running as a competitive sport and healthful exercise. The RRCA's mission is to represent and promote the common interests of its member clubs and individual runners through education, leadership, and other services.

D.C.-Area Racing

The Washington, D.C., racing community is large, friendly, and encouraging to racers at all levels. Most races benefit charitable organizations, such as the Race for the Cure—the largest 5K in the country, which helps provide awareness of and fund research in breast cancer. Find a charity you support and run for it. Whether you are competitive or not, you will have fun. Not to mention the chance to expand your T-shirt wardrobe! There are a lot of races in the area; below you'll find a few of the more interesting ones. For running tips, race entry forms, and a complete listing of races for the year, check out *Race Packet* or *Run Washington*. Paper versions can be picked up in many running stores, or you can get a subscription.

▶ Race Packet *Subscriptions*

P. O. Box 25049, Arlington, VA 22202; www.race packet.com

▶ The Washington Running Report

13710 Ashby Road, Rockville, MD 20853; (301) 871–0005; www.runwashington.com

Great Local Races

▶ *AIDS Walk—Washington, D.C.*

www.aidswalkwashington.org

In the city with the highest incidence of AIDS per capita in the country, it is obvious that AIDS education and funding are desperately needed. Lend some support to those who live with this terrible disease. The walk takes place on the National Mall usually on a Saturday in the beginning of October. Money is raised for the HIV/AIDS programs of Whitman-Walker Clinic—the primary community-based provider of HIV and AIDS services in the D.C. area, including HIV primary medical, dental, and ophthalmology services, mental health counseling, legal services, case management, and a food bank. Even if you're not walking, donations are welcome. Registration takes place in September, and all who register receive an AIDS Walk T-shirt. Registration can be completed online, at one of the area Whitman-Walker Clinics, or at a number of local malls and stores.

5K RACES

The 5K (3.1 miles) is the most popular racing distance in America. Getting in shape for a 5K can be a motivational goal or a good test of speed for the more advanced runner. There are races almost every weekend in the Washington area. A listing of most of these can be found in the back of the Weekend section of the *Washington Post*. An easy, but thorough, guide to train for your first 5K can be found at the *Runner's World* site: www.runnersworld.com.

▶ *Run vs. Row 10K Challenge & 4K Walk*

Alexandria Boat House (blue-and-white building), 1 Madison Street, Alexandria, VA

Along the waterfront in Old Town Alexandria, a unique race occurs every spring that's fun for runners, walkers, and spectators. Runners race against the T. C. Williams High School varsity crew teams rowing on the river. The race benefits the Alexandria Crew Boosters Club (a nonprofit organization), which in turn provides support and services to the rowing program and offers scholarships.

The event occurs at the end of March—usually the last Saturday. The running race starts at the corner of Union and Pendleton Streets, next to the Alexandria Boat House and Oronoco Bay Park. While participants run along the Potomac, crew teams from West Potomac, Yorktown, and St. Albans usually join in on the river. The walkers go the 4K (2.5 miles) to Jones Point and back.

To register, contact the boathouse, Pacers (running store) in Alexandria, or www.racepacket.com, www.runvsrow.com, or info@runvsrow.com.

To get there: The Alexandria Community Rowing (ACR) Boat House is the only boathouse in Virginia—about 7 miles downstream from Georgetown, and located at the end of Madison Street in Old Town Alexandria. From Route 1, turn onto Madison Street heading toward the river. Take Madison Street all the way to the end, at the Potomac River. Public parking is available—please do not park in the condo development on your left.

▶ The Army 10 Miler

www.armytenmiler.com

The Army 10 Miler is—with almost 20,000 racers—the world's largest 10-mile race. It starts out at the Pentagon, crosses Memorial Bridge, goes up to Capitol Hill, and then returns to the Pentagon for the finish. The best spectator locations are Memorial Bridge, the Health and Human Services Building (Independence and 3rd), and the finish line at the Pentagon North Parking Lot. There are some restrictions for security reasons: You must maintain at least a sixteen-minute-mile pace in order for everyone to finish on time and clear the bridges. No bags, backpacks, bikes, in-line skates, skateboards, or joggers' baby strollers. The course is limited to runners, wheelchair athletes, and officials. There are water stations every 2 miles, and post-race refreshments are available for the runners. Please observe all barricades and signs.

There is also a Junior 10-Miler Fun Run for kids from kindergarten through eighth grade. The race is not longer than a 1K run. Parents or legal guardians must complete a registration for any child entering.

The Army 10 Miler usually takes place in the middle of October. Unfortunately, the 2001 race had to be canceled due to the September 11 tragedy. Future races are still being planned. Registrations can be mailed in or completed online. Online registration opens in early spring. No on-site registrations. Proceeds from the race support soldiers and soldier family programs.

If you are new to the Army 10 Miler, please e-mail your name, address, and the number of brochures (entry forms) needed to armytenmiler@fmmc.army.mil.

▶ National Race for the Cure

Komen National Race for the Cure, 1911 North Fort Myer Drive, Suite 112, Arlington, VA 22209; (703) 848–8884; www.nationalraceforthecure.com

The Washington, D.C., Race for the Cure is the largest 5K in the country—there are typically about 70,000 participants. It's part of the Komen Race for the Cure Series, the largest series of 5K runs/fitness walks in the world. The 5K run/walk and 1-mile fun walk benefit breast cancer research, education, screening, and treatment programs. A national toll-free breast health care line is available at (800) I'M–AWARE (800–462–9273).

The Race for the Cure takes place on the first Saturday in June on the Washington Monument grounds. There is no registration on race day. Parking is pretty difficult on race day, so try to take the Metro if possible—there's free parking at Metro-operated lots on weekends. Take the Red, Orange, or Blue line to Metro Center, or take the Orange or Blue line to the Federal Triangle or Smithsonian Metro stations.

▶ The Marine Corps Marathon

P. O. Box 188, Quantico, VA, 22134; (703) 784–2225 or (800) RUN–USMC; www.marinemarathon.com

Often called the People's Marathon because it's the only major open-registration marathon in the United States, this amateur race begins and ends at the Marine Corps War Memorial (Iwo Jima Monument). Runners start to the blast of a 105-millimeter howitzer—what else would you expect from the marines? The race goes through Arlington, Georgetown, and Washington as well as by many monuments and

Marines run past the tulips in spring.

- **Halloween.** There are a number of Halloween races (10K, 5K, and shorter fun runs/walks) offered around D.C., and people often dress up in costume for the races.
- **Jingle Bell Race.** Usually held the weekend after Thanksgiving, the Jingle Bell Race is basically a Christmas race, but it's held early enough to avoid the ice and snow—yet late enough for the weather to be really cold. Organizers give out jingle bells (tiny sleigh bells) to all runners, who tie them to their shoelaces. It sounds like Santa himself is coming your way as the runners jingle down the streets.

For complete listings of Halloween and Jingle Bell races, check out www.racepacket.com.

memorials. The course is USA Track & Field certified as 26 miles and 385 yards—a regulation marathon course. While most of the course is flat, there is one last hill at the end . . . again, what else would you expect from the corps?

Because the marathon is open, there are many more people who want to run than the 16,000 slots available. Registration starts in February and usually continues until May. Then a lottery determines who gets those 16,000 slots. No unauthorized bicycles, roller skates, or Walkmans are permitted. Check the Web site for more information. The Marine Corps Marathon is run every year on the fourth Sunday in October.

▶ The Washington DC Marathon

H2O Entertainment Group, Arlington, VA; (703) 528–8176; www.washingtondcmarathon. com

The Marine Corps Marathon is a Washington institution and, given its longtime status as the only marathon in the area, amazingly popular. As a result, it has become more and more difficult to get entered over the years. The Washington DC Marathon was developed to fill this gap and give runners another chance to run through the beautiful streets of Washington—this time, in spring. Begun in 2002, the marathon is held each year at the end of March—coinciding with the start of the annual International Cherry Blossom Festival. It's a beautiful course, starting at Memorial Bridge.

Participants must be sixteen years or older on race day. The closest Metro station to the start is the Arlington Cemetery stop on the Blue line. Walkers and "back-of-the-pack" runners are welcome, but they should know that vehicular traffic will eventually reopen along the course—at which time slower participants need to move to the side.

Despite having only a few races under its belt, the Washington DC Marathon seems to be a very well-run organization. The course is USA Track & Field certified; incline has been removed from it to make the route flatter and faster. Complete information and online registration can be found on the Web site.

Running Clubs

Trying to train for a race, or to get motivated—or just looking to meet some more runners? Join a running club. There are many in the capital region. If you can't find one in your area, contact the Road Runners Club of America (RRCA) at www.rrca.org; this group also has information on how to start a running club in your area. Here are a few clubs that belong to the RRCA in the D.C. metro area:

Virginia

▶ DC Road Runners

P. O. Box 1352, Arlington, VA 22210; evening (703) 486–1466; day (202) 675–6322; www.dcroadrunners.org

▶ Fleet Feet Runners

7516 Leesburg Pike, Falls Church, VA 22043; evening (703) 476–9067; day (703) 790–3338

▶ Loudoun Road Runners

P. O. Box 3342, Leesburg, VA 20177; (540) 882–3641; www.loudounroadrunners.org

▶ Marine Corps Marathon

P. O. Box 188, Quantico, VA 22134; (703) 784–2225; www.marinemarathon.com

▶ Northern Virginia Running Club

2830 Monroe Street, Falls Church, VA 22042; (703) 532–8031; www.novarun.com

▶ Reston Runners

P. O. Box 2924, Reston, VA 22090; (703) 435–FOOT; www.restonrunners.org

▶ RidgeRunners Club

12400 Oakwood Drive, Lake Ridge, VA 22192; (703) 497–7113; lakeridgerunners.tripod.com

▶ Virginia Happy Trails R.C.

8396 Idylwood Road, Vienna, VA 22182; evening (703) 560–6304; day (202) 885–1610; www.vhtrc.org

▶ Washington Runhers Unlimited

P. O. Box 5622, Arlington, VA 22205; (703) 548–3507; www.washingtonrunhers.org

Washington Runhers is a club founded in 1976 to promote women's running in the D.C. metro area.

Maryland

▶ Montgomery County Road Runners Club

P. O. Box 1703, Rockville, MD 20849; (301) 353–0200; www.mcrrc.org

▶ Prince George's Running Club

P. O. Box 877, Greenbelt, MD 20768; (301) 486–0041; www.pgrc.org

▶ Howard County Striders

P. O. Box 563, Columbia, MD 21045; (410) 964–1998; www.striders.net

▶ Goddard Run & Orienteering

NASA GSFC Code 313, Greenbelt, MD 20771; evening (301) 776–7069; day (301) 286–8061

▶ Frederick Steeplechasers

P. O. Box 681, Frederick, MD 21705-0681; (301) 694–3456; members.aol.com/FSRCWeb

▶ Chesapeake Bay Running Club

P. O. Box 293, Patuxent River, MD 20670; (301) 737–0187; www.smliving.com/cbrc

▶ Cherry Blossom Inc.

18476 Stone Hollow Drive, Germantown, MD 20874; (301) 320–6865; cherryblossom.org

▶ Capitol Hill Runners

1104 Sanford Lane, Accokeek, MD 20607; evening (301) 283–0821

▶ Annapolis Striders

P. O. Box 187, Annapolis, MD 21401; (410) 268–1165; annapolisstriders.org

4 Climbing

CLIMBING HAS A LOT TO OFFER. There probably isn't another sport out there that demands such a combination of physical and mental awareness—and you have to be in shape for both to climb well. As you climb, you know exactly where every part of your body is and where your weight is placed at all times. You twist and maneuver your body up a rock while constantly fighting the forces of gravity. It's ballet and battle wrapped up in one. Even the beginner can find a high level of satisfaction.

Obviously, you should carefully consider the risks involved before embarking on any sort of climbing. I won't sugarcoat it: You can die when climbing. Accidents happen every year ending in broken bones, paralysis, and, yes, even death. Even bouldering around on a small rock where you are just a few feet off the ground can result in serious injury. Don't go climbing before weighing all these facts thoroughly.

Different Kinds of Climbing

■ *Bouldering* involves climbing over and around boulders or just climbing low—a few feet up in the air. Transversing across a rock can be just as challenging as climbing up the rock. You can practice your techniques without roping up. But be aware that you can still hurt yourself if you fall even from a few feet. Make sure you have a safe landing zone and a spotter. Twisted and broken ankles are a real risk. Make sure you're wearing a helmet at all times. No, there's not a big likelihood of falling debris, but you don't want to fall on your bare head.

■ *Toproping* is often used when climbing shorter cliffs. An anchor system is tied to the top of the cliff, and the ropes hang down through carabiners in an inverted V. A climber ties into one end of the rope while the other end is tended (belayed) by another climber. The person on belay takes the slack out of the rope and makes sure the climber doesn't hit the ground. Proper belaying takes training and close attention to the climber. Toproping allows a climber to develop both climbing techniques and belaying skills.

■ *Lead climbing* is done on longer climbs where you can't anchor your rope at the top—or choose not to. A lead climber, tied to a rope, goes up the rock, putting in pieces of gear (protection), which are then clipped to carabiners along the way. The rope slides freely through the protection and, in the event of a fall, serves to shorten the potential distance. The bottom climber belays. When the lead climber gets to a solid stopping point, he constructs a solid anchor of gear and ties in. The former belayer now climbs up the rock following the rope and cleaning the gear the leader placed earlier. The team continues up in this fashion until the top of the climb is reached. A climb becomes "multipitch" once the length of the climb is greater than the length of the rope.

■ *Ice climbing* is climbing . . . ice. Ice is formed by frozen waterfalls, or by rain and snowmelt that freeze over cliffs. Ice climbs may form as far south as North Carolina, but they're far more reliable in and around New England. Special equipment such as crampons, ice picks, and other tools are used. Save for the gear, the technical techniques aren't terribly different from other climbing. Due to the highly specialized gear and nature of ice climbing, however, professional instruction is highly recommended.

■ *Alpine climbing* is a specialized discipline that involves moving quickly over rock, snow, and ice. It's high-mountain climbing that requires special equipment and training and isn't for the beginner.

■ *Mountaineering,* on the other hand, requires only some basic instruction and a reasonable level of fitness. While involving some of the same equipment (ice ax and crampons), mountaineering is a different breed of climbing than the sometimes more technical disciplines of rock and ice.

Usually when people learn to climb, they start with bouldering or toproping, working on climbing techniques and belaying skills. Then they move on to lead climbing and, occasionally, to ice or alpine climbing. One nice thing about basic climbing is that after the initial (and sometimes steep) start-up costs, climbing is nearly free—a nice change from other sports.

Climbers practice toproping and belaying at Carderock Park in Potomac, Maryland.

Beginner's Gear List

The kind of climbing you are doing may determine a lot of your gear as well as the kind of ropes you will need. Lead climbing may demand different gear than does toproping; rappellers may not use the same rope as climbers. But there are a few things that every climber needs.

- Helmet.
- Harness. Make sure it fits properly, and never buy any used nylon climbing gear.
- Climbing shoes. Have someone help you get some climbing shoes that fit properly. You don't want your feet to be able to move within the shoe, because you may need to use a toe to support your entire weight. These shoes aren't really made for walking, but you don't want them so tight that they cut off your circulation. Still, stiffness is good. Walking around in them is bad for them, as is leaving them in hot places (like a car). Also, a clean shoe will help you keep your grip on the rocks. Don't let them get dusty and dirty.
- Chalk bag. Some experienced climbers think this isn't necessary—but especially as a beginner, chalk really does help keep your hands dry and able to grip.
- Belay device. There are a few variations. Ask someone knowledgeable about the differences.
- Two locking D carabiners.

Looking for an Instructor

Climbing can result in serious injury or death. You climb at your own risk. You must be responsible for every one of your actions. Finding a good instructor is crucial. There are too many people on the rocks who don't know what they're doing because they were never trained properly. These people are at the greatest risk of injury. An instructor should be able to teach you the proper techniques and explain the theory behind the teaching. Look for an instructor or company with extensive experience—and realize that you get what you pay for. Make sure the firm is fully insured and offers extensive training for staff. See if it's recognized by its peers as a leader in the field.

▶ Earth Treks Climbing Center

7125-C Columbia Gateway Drive, Columbia, MD 21046; (410) 465–5492 or (800) CLIMB–UP; www.earthtreksclimbing.com

Chris Warner began teaching in the D.C. area back in 1990 and his company, Earth Treks, has grown ever since. Earth Treks has taught thousands of aspiring and experienced climbers and mountaineers. The only accredited guide service in the area, it's certified by the American Mountain Guides Association (AMGA) and the state

GIRLS VERSUS BOYS; TALL VERSUS SHORT

Don't make the mistake of thinking you're too short or not strong enough to climb; this isn't a sport only for tall men with lots of upper-body strength. Climbers should be using their legs to push themselves up and their arms to guide them—kind of like climbing a ladder. They shouldn't be pulling themselves up the entire rock route with their arms. Sometimes you'll work your arms and need some "oomph" to get by. But if you're doing an entry-level climb and your arms are tired by the end of the route, you're probably doing it wrong.

Flexibility, the ability to control your body position, and shifting your weight are all critical. Women and kids do very well in the sport. Yes, it's true that having some height makes it easier to reach those crevices, nooks, knobs, and various other handholds. A tall climber may be able to bypass an overhang in a couple of moves while it may take a shorter climber a few more. On the other hand, there are many climbs where body position is necessarily cramped and lack of height is a definite advantage. Being shorter also forces you to become more creative with your routes and can improve technique. It often makes for a better climber in the long run.

of Maryland. Employees go through an intense education program—first staff training, then shadow training where they observe, followed by assisting; only then can they become lead instructors. Employees also undergo ten days of internal training a year—which is a lot—and must meet a thorough skills checklist.

Earth Treks offers rock and ice climbing instruction, mountaineering guide services, an indoor climbing center, a private teaching and conference center, equipment rental, and 10,000 square feet of vertical climbing surface.

▶ Seneca Rocks Climbing School

P. O. Box 53, Seneca Rocks, WV 26884-0053; (304) 567–2600 or (800) 548–0108; www.seneca-rocks.com/climbing.links.html

Another excellent climbing school in the area is Seneca Rocks Climbing School. The folks here teach at Seneca Rocks in West Virginia. Seneca Rocks is a more technical climb than climbing around the Potomac. The climbing school is located behind Harper's Store on Route 33.

▶ Seneca Rocks Mountain Guides and Outfitters

Route 33, Seneca Rocks, WV; (800) 451–5108 or (304) 567–2117

This school also has an excellent reputation and has helped climbers experience new views of the world. Seneca Rocks Mountain Guides is located across the street from Harper's Store on Route 33.

Local Climbs

There are a few good climbs in the D.C. area, all best for toproping. You have the choice of either Great Falls or Carderock. The rock itself is different in the two places, which will give you a different climbing experience. For more information on each climb area, see below.

▶ Great Falls

Great Falls National Park—Virginia, 9200 Old Dominion Drive, Great Falls, VA 22066; (703) 285–2965; www.nps.gov/gwmp/grfa/

Great Falls Park—Maryland, Potomac, MD; (301) 767–3714

Great Falls has vertical-to-overhanging faces, resulting in a more power-oriented way of climbing. The area offers climbs from beginner to advanced.

Great Falls is a great local climbing location—with an amazing view of the Potomac River as well. The Potomac cuts through the rock, creating the famous falls that are beautiful any time of year, along with Mather Gorge. Climbers enjoy the cliffs of this gorge on both sides of the river. People climb anytime except when the water

Climbers reach the top at Carderock Park, a great spot for beginning climbers.

is exceptionally high. Be careful after big rains. Do not disturb any roping systems that you see along the top. There is a sign-in book for climbers at the visitor center. It's not required, but it's a good idea to let the park service know how many people are on the rocks—and you can use it to see if your friends are out there.

People do climb on the Maryland side of Great Falls, but the majority use the Virginia side, which offers easier accessibility and more climbs to choose from. From the Maryland side you can follow the wooden walkways across the islands to Olmstead Island, where you can watch the climbers on the Virginia side. Great Falls is the closest Washington climbing location after Carderock; both parks are about 12 miles from D.C. There are nice picnic areas at both, so you can enjoy a full day climbing at the falls.

Great Falls National Park on the Virginia side closes at dusk; the visitor center is open daily 10:00 A.M. to 5:00 P.M. Admission is about $4.00 for noncommercial vehicles. Take exit 13 off the Beltway to Georgetown Pike, go west for 4.3 miles, then turn right onto Old Dominion Drive into the park.

To reach the Maryland side, take the Beltway to exit 39 onto Route 190 (River Road northbound). After 7 miles, a road leading left will mark the entrance to the park.

WHAT'S THE PROBLEM WITH CLIMBERS?

According to Chris Warner of Earth Treks, the biggest problem with climbers in the capital area is a lack of education. Understanding the theory behind both equipment and safety techniques is critical. Too often people who really don't know what they're doing teach other people—which just passes along improper and unsafe practices. Take a class from folks who know what they're doing!

Setting up a proper toprope anchor system is another huge problem. Walking up and down the clifftop trails at Great Falls, you can see lots of climbers who don't understand how to perform this basic yet critical task.

Improper belaying—really, an attentiveness issue—is a big concern for Chris. And finally, not wearing a helmet is always a problem.

▶ *Carderock Park*

Potomac, MD

Carderock is more user-friendly for beginners. It's the best site for toproping in the area, offering climbs for beginners to advanced. Carderock has less-than-vertical faces; your climbing movements will be more delicate, and you'll have to be stronger on technique.

To reach Carderock Park, follow the directions for the Maryland side of Great Falls. Take the Beltway to exit 39 onto Route 190 (River Road northbound). From

River Road northbound, take the David Taylor Naval Research Center exit and take a left across the bridge away from the entrance to the base. You'll be taken right into the park. You'll probably want to park in the lots farthest to your right.

For More Information

Check out Indy's underground climbing guide to Sugarloaf Mountain: www.bcpl. net/~ indy/climbing/guide.html.

Chris Warner's Picks

Chris Warner, founder of Earth Treks, is one of the great treasures of the Washington, D.C., area. A long-standing member of the D.C. climbing community, he has shared his experiences with local radio stations and schoolchildren in our area. He is one of fifteen people in the country certified as an alpine guide and recently climbed to the summit of Everest after a lifetime of preparation. You can follow the experiences of Chris and his team from the journals on their Web site (www.earthtreksclimbing. com). Climbing mountains like Everest and K2 makes for some amazing adventure reading—a must for all climbers.

When I e-mailed Chris for his help with the book, he responded with his laptop from high atop a Himalayan peak: "Can't a man hide in Tibet anymore?" He was cultivating his yak herding techniques, but took a break long enough to offer some opinions on area climbing.

■ *Best local climbing:* Carderock Park on the Potomac, just downstream from Great Falls. This is also a fun spot to hike along the clifftops. Once again, don't climb when the water is extremely high, be careful after big rains, and do not disturb any roping systems that you see along the top.

■ *Best day-trip climbing:* the Hermitage. Right on the Appalachian Trail (Schaffer Rock), the Hermitage is a cabin owned by the Potomac Appalachian Trail Club just over the border in southern Pennsylvania, near Michaux State Forest. It's a nice, less advanced climb, and not too crowded. There's a beautiful hemlock grove along the stream.

■ *Best weekend destination for climbing:* Seneca Rocks, West Virginia. Known as the place to learn multipitch climbing in the D.C. area, Seneca Rocks also has a lot to offer advanced climbers outside the D.C. area. There are two peaks, the South Peak and North Peak, and each has an East and West Face. The South Peak is the only place in the East that requires technical roped climbing to reach its summit—the next closest spot for this is Devil's Tower in Wyoming. There are campgrounds, cabins, and motels in the area so you can be as woodsy as you want to be.

Other Fun Places to Climb

▪ *Caudy's Castle.* Another cool place—a good day trip with advanced climbing. Caudy's Castle is a rock formation on the Cacapon River in West Virginia's scenic eastern panhandle region—specifically, west of Winchester, Virginia. The Cacapon River, as part of the Potomac River watershed, is an American Heritage River.

▪ *Old Rag Mountain,* Shenandoah National Park. Good climbing—and good hiking, too, if you're with a mixed group for a day. Exit Skyline Drive at Thornton Gap, mile 31.5. The hike begins at the bottom of the mountain instead of from Skyline Drive. Despite the tough, steep climb to the summit, this is one of the most popular hikes in Shenandoah National Park and in Virginia. Enjoy the amazing views, but realize that hikers over the age of sixteen now pay a fee to climb Old Rag. A collection box is at the trailhead.

▪ *Crescent Rocks* overlook the Shenandoah River in Virginia; they're found near Snickers Gap out toward Purcellville. Parking may be prohibited. You can access the cliffs from the Appalachian Trail.

5 Biking

UNLIKE MANY CITIES around the country, Washington, D.C.'s business districts and community living are located in close proximity. There are short distances between business, shopping, and homes—which make biking a real transportation alternative. There are probably few cities with as many biking clubs, few metropolitan areas with as many bike trails, and few places that are as beautiful and enjoyable as Washington. Whether biking the monuments or enjoying one of the roads in Rock Creek Park that are closed to traffic, Washington is a real gem for bikers.

Purchasing a Bicycle

Purchasing a bicycle has changed over the years. Remember the days when Schwinn was king? No one knew what a mountain bike was fifteen years ago, and now they make up 58 percent of all bike sales. Rather than just jumping on a trend, think about the kind of riding you'll be doing before you decide on a bike. If you'll be riding only the mountains or rough terrain—you're obviously looking for a mountain bike. If you're only commuting through the streets—you may want a road-racing bike. For leisurely rides out on smooth trails—you may want a cruiser. Going for tricks in your neighbor's backyard pool? Go for a BMX. Combinations may demand a hybrid. Don't forget to budget for a helmet that fits properly!

A good bike store can steer you in the right direction. Ask lots of questions, and find a shop willing to take the time to go over everything with you. Frames and components (brakes, shocks, gears, shifters, seat, handlebar, even the pedals) are very important; look closely until you find the combination you want.

Take a test ride. Try the bike out and see how it performs. Take into account the comfort of the seat, how the bike shifts, how it brakes, even the ease of turning.

Sizing—Bike Fit

Make sure the bike you purchase fits—a good bike store can help you with that, too. You don't want a bike that's too big or too small. Both can impact performance, speed, comfort, and safety.

Sizing bikes varies from type to type. For road bikes, you should have at least an inch of clearance between the top tube and your crotch as you stand astride the bike. Clearance for a hybrid or cross bike should be about 2 inches. Sizing for a mountain bike is a little different. The clearance should be 3 to 4 inches.

When sitting square on the seat, put your foot on the pedal at the lowest position the pedal can be. Your leg should be bent a little. When pedaling, your leg should not be fully extended. You should be able to just lean forward with your hands comfortably on the handlebars—you shouldn't be reaching out for them. If they seem too close in, the bike may not fit right. A bike shop can help you make adjustments to the handlebar stem or move the seat back.

Kinds of Bikes

■ *Tandem bikes.* Yep, these are the two-seaters—for people who really like each other and don't ever have the need to explore on their own. Okay, seriously, they're kind of fun. You can even get a tandem extension (half a bike) that will attach to the seat-post of your existing bike. The extra set of pedals makes your ride that much easier.
■ *Recumbent bikes.* Here, you sit on the bike as you would in a chair—sort of the La-Z-Boy of the biking world. With the pedals in front, you can push out using your back as support. You can actually reach pretty decent speeds and ride for a long time, but it's definitely a different feeling and center of balance than normal bikes. You're also a little lower, and your head is at the back of the bike instead of leaning forward. Your view will be different from a regular bicyclist's—something to consider when you're moving about town. Remember that recumbents are not as visible to motorists, either.
■ *Mountain bikes.* These are probably the most popular models in recent years, and not a bad choice for urban riding considering all the potholes. If you're using your mountain bike on the mean streets, you may want to switch to slick tires. The wide knobby models that usually come with mountain bikes slow you down and aren't as good for steering as slicks. With all the quick-switch wheels out there, you could have two sets of rims with knobby and slick tires; biking to work or biking to the mountains would then require just an easy switch. Simply having a slick back tire makes a huge difference on pavement. Most good biking stores can find something to suit your situation.

- *Road-racing bikes.* They're fast, they're fun—just make sure you get a good fit when you purchase one. Fit is crucial if you're to get the most out of your rides, and it's even more important with road-racing bikes. Road racers aren't for offroading.

- *Cruisers.* Take a long ride along the C&O Canal with a cruiser. No fancy gear shifts or brakes that you have to worry about breaking—just the traditional big bike with one gear. You turn the pedal backward to brake. They're sturdy bikes with very comfortable seats, and they make for long rides on some of the local trails. On the downside, they don't take hills very well.

- *Hybrids.* Perhaps the most underrated, underappreciated bikes out there, hybrids are probably what people should be purchasing about 80 percent of the time. They come in many different types—you can find a model to use on the city streets, or one to take on a dirt road excursion. Maybe they're not ready for riding down Everest, but they are surprisingly sturdy and comfortable. As always, ask a lot of questions to find a hybrid that's right for you.

- *BMX bikes.* These bikes are built for dirt tracks and jumps, with wider tires for better traction and to handle the bumps more easily. Easy to ride, they offer a single gear for simple fun. They're popular with preteens—but the BMX crowds don't seem to want to give up their bikes as they get older. And their popularity is rising because of the X Games and stars like Dave Mirra showing all the amazing tricks that can be performed on these bikes.

For More Information

To check out all kinds of bike reviews, visit www.bikereviews.com.

Getting Ready to Ride

Clothing

Prepare yourself for the elements. If you're riding at 20 miles an hour, the wind will make a cool day seem a lot cooler. Use layers, wear a windbreaker, and remember, no loose clothing around your legs so nothing can get caught in the chain. Cycling pants and shorts have pads in them to make the ride that much more comfortable—

CHEAP BIKES!

Looking for a good bike cheap? Call your local police station and ask about police auctions. Many great bikes that are found or stolen are sold really cheap at these auctions. They're especially good places to pick up kids' bikes—and the kids don't care if it's used, they just want a bike! The auction itself can make a fun family outing, too.

and they work! If you're riding on a cold day, try a helmet liner for under your helmet (it's too hard to put a hat on over it). If it's too warm or if you get warmer as you ride, you can just take off some of the layers.

Traffic and Biking Safety

- A bike is considered a vehicle and has the same right-of-way as a motor vehicle. Always ride single file in the same direction as other vehicles. Never ride against traffic.
- On busy roads and in traffic, always be visible. Use a flag or wear an orange vest, and put reflectors on your bike.
- Use hand signals.
- Always wear a helmet. It should fit snugly on your head and securely on your forehead. Readjust the straps each time you wear the helmet.
- Obey all regulatory signs and traffic lights.
- Use a bell so pedestrians know when you're passing.
- Use lights at night. Headlights are required by law at night, but taillights are a good addition as well.
- Be alert.
- Ride defensively.
- Keep both hands ready to brake.
- Be visible.
- Be aware—cars may seemingly come out of nowhere.
- Watch out for bumps and gravel along the side of the road.
- Always be aware of the surface you're riding on.
- Look out for parked cars opening their doors or cars cutting you off.
- Scan the road behind you.

The District of Columbia, Maryland, and Virginia have different laws for bicycle position, passing cars, turning left, restricted roads, cycling on sidewalks, mandatory use of bike paths and lanes, helmets, and lights. Make sure you know your local laws.

For the name and number of an instructor near you, contact the League of American Bicyclists (see "Biking Organizations and Group Trips," later in this chapter).

Road Repairs

No one likes a flat tire, but it happens. Welcome to reality! Picture this—you go out for a nice two-hour bike ride with a friend. At the apex of the ride, one hour out, you get a flat. If you're ill equipped, you'll spend the next two hours just walking your bike home. Your friend will either dump you and continue to enjoy the day, or will be cursing your name during the two hours back.

Be prepared before you go out so a simple flat is a ten-minute fix instead of a daylong ordeal. Ask your bike shop about which tools you need and some of the more common problems. Practice making basic repairs before you head out. Remember, it's difficult to make repairs when you're stuck and have never done it before.

A tool kit fits under the seat of your bike. Tool kits usually include:

- Crescent wrench.
- Screwdriver.
- Tire patch kit.
- Allen wrenches, if you have special bolts on your bike.
- Tire irons. These help you take out the tube without damaging the tire.

Ride to Work—Metro

There are almost 20,000 work-related bike trips in our region each day. Riding to work costs less than driving or taking transit. If you hadn't noticed, just about every county around has recently expanded the bike lanes on its roads and biking paths in the hope that more people will get on their bikes and off the road. If you want to start biking to work, try a practice run on a Saturday or Sunday and see how it goes. You'll get a feeling for whether or not it's feasible. If you like it, try it just one day a week, like on a Friday. It may take a few tries during the week to find your best route or time to ride. The Washington Area Bicyclists Association's commuter mentor program will put you in touch with other people in your area who bike to work and can help you find the most comfortable route; call (202) 628–2500 or visit www.waba.org.

Bus It

Since December 2002 bicycle racks have been mounted on the front of every Metro bus. (Most Montgomery County "RIDE ON" buses already had bike racks). Each rack holds two bikes. Let

BIKE SECURITY— LOCKS

Let's face facts—whether or not you spent a lot of cash for your bike, no one wants to have a bike stolen. Locks are the best way to help prevent theft. Notice that I said *help* prevent theft. There is no theftproof lock out on the market. Thieves find ways. But you can do your best to mitigate the risk. Here are some tips that *may* help:

- Lock your bike in a place that's secure—inside a building if possible.
- If you're locking it outdoors, lock your frame and both wheels to an immovable object. Don't lock a bike to a sign or anything that can be easily unbolted, bent, cut, or removed.
- Pick a place that's well lit and well traveled.
- If your seat is quick release, take it with you.
- If you have a trip computer on your bike, take it with you.
- Don't leave things on your bike that are easy to take off if you don't want them stolen.
- U-locks seem to be the sturdiest and most secure.
- Try using two different types of locks—say, one U-shaped lock, plus a cable lock. Thieves need different tools for each type of lock. More locks require more time to pick, and that puts a thief at greater risk of getting caught.

the bus driver know you'll be using the rack and just follow the instructions posted on the front of the rack. Bus to the Metro, to work, shopping, or sight-seeing downtown.

Metro Station Facilities

Biking directly to work isn't always an option for people, but biking to the Metro often is. Many Metro stations have facilities for bicycle storage (racks and rental lockers) so you can ride your bicycle to a station, leave it there, and take Metrorail. Racks are free on a first-come, first-served basis. Have a good lock (standard, medium, key padlock). A list of stations that have racks and lockers is available at any station. Ask the stationmaster if you don't see a brochure outside. For locker rental, call (202) 962–1116.

Taking Your Bike on the Metro Train

Okay, so you want to ride to the Metro but don't want to leave your bike there . . . just take your bike with you on the train! Of course, there are a few rules you'll have to follow:

- Bikes are permitted weekdays *except* 7:00 to 10:00 A.M. and 4:00 to 7:00 P.M. There's a limit of two bicycles per train.
- Bikes are permitted all day Saturday, Sunday, and most holidays—limit four bicycles per train. (They're not permitted on July 4 or other large crowd days.)
- Only regular-sized bikes—no tricycles or training wheels.
- The maximum size is 80 inches long, 48 inches high, and 22 inches wide.
- Anyone under sixteen years must be accompanied by an adult.
- Always use the elevator, never the escalators.
- Don't block doorways or aisles.
- Yield to other passengers.
- *Never* ride bicycles in stations, on platforms, or on trains.
- Keep both wheels on the ground, keep the kickstand up, and always have control.
- When on the Metro, enter through the first and last doors—not the center emergency doors.
- In an emergency, put your bicycle on the seats (out of the path of passengers) and leave it on the train.

For More Information

- www.biketowork.com is a site dedicated to bicycle commuting.
- You can find a copy of the Metro *Bike-On-Rail Guidelines* at any stations and most commuter stores, or see the Metro Web site: www.wmata.com/metrorail/bikeon rails.htm.

Street Biking Around Washington

The neighborhood streets are always the most popular places to bike, but they're not always the safest as our area gets congested with more and more traffic. Check out the many trails around the city. In other words, check out chapter 1, "Trails," then go outside and play.

▶ Rock Creek Park Car-Free Zones

www.rockcreekpark.net

About 4 miles of the park's roadways are car-free for recreational use on weekends and holidays. Great for bike outings and teaching the little ones to ride! The car-free zones include Bingham Drive, Sherrill Drive, and three sections of Beach Drive.

Mountain Biking Around Washington

Mountain biking is fun, but realize that many of the trails in the area are mulituse trails and are also used by horseback riders, walkers, runners, hikers, and people out for a casual stroll. Follow the rules of the trail. Ask permission before passing those on horseback. Unauthorized trail building and things like ramps and jumps are against the law. If you want to build some trails, you should contact an organization such as MORE (see "Biking Organizations and Group Trips," later in this chapter) for information on trail building projects.

Keep safety as your primary goal. Make sure you can come back to ride the trail another day! Know your limitations and know the trail—get a map if possible. You don't want to be rounding a bend and not realize there's a cliff there. And always remember, if you come to a spot that's technically challenging, don't be afraid to dismount and walk your bike around the obstacle. Better safe than sorry.

Let's face facts—the sport of mountain biking was almost nonexistent just fifteen years ago. Today, about 58 percent of the bicycles sold in the United States are mountain bikes. The increasing numbers of mountain bike owners in the Baltimore/ Washington region are all searching for nearby locations to cycle.

Some people are willing to drive out to rural Loudoun or western Maryland to find unpaved roads. Others are willing to go farther—say, out to West Virginia—in order to ride the fire roads through the Shenandoah Mountains. All very fun, but there are some excellent singletracks, fire roads, and paved paths closer to home. Check out the biking maps to find a good location near you. Here are a few locations that you may want to check out.

Washington, D.C.

▶ Rock Creek Park

While bikes aren't allowed on the unpaved trails around the park, the paved trails that parallel Oregon Avenue, Military Road, and Bingham Drive are challenging. See the "Rock Creek Park" map and chapter 1, "Trails," for more details.

▶ Fort Dupont Park

Randle Circle, SE, Washington, DC; (202) 426–7723; www.nps.gov/fodu

A heavily wooded park with numerous trails running through its 376 acres, Fort Dupont was built in 1861 to guard against Confederate attacks—one of the sixty-four forts surrounding Washington during the Civil War. It's open dawn to dusk.

Virginia

▶ Conway Robinson State Forest

You'll find about 5 miles of multiuse trails here. Go out I–66 and take the second right (exit 29) northbound.

▶ Fountainhead Regional Park

10876 Hampton Road, Fairfax Station, VA 22039

The mountain biking trail is open year-round on the 5-plus miles of trails.

▶ George Washington National Forest

Elizabeth Furnace area. Go out I–66 and take exit 6 at Front Royal/Winchester.

▶ Lake Accotink and Wakefield Park Trail System

Located in Annandale, Virginia, the parks are several miles apart and separated by Braddock Road. A path takes you under Braddock Road and joins the two trail systems. Accotink, around the lake, is probably the easier for riding. But Accotink's trails go farther. Wakefield, on the other hand, is much more challenging. You can link up to the Wakefield trails by going down to the recycling bins at the farthest end of the parking lot. The trails are behind the park—behind the tennis courts. Lots of great hills behind Wakefield.

To reach Lake Accotink, exit the Beltway on Braddock Road and drive 1.5 miles east. Turn right onto Backlick Road, which splits and becomes Amherst Avenue; turn right onto Essex Avenue. Drive down not quite a mile and park near the intersection with Middlesex Avenue. The entrance to the park is marked by a sign that says NO MOTOR VEHICLES. Follow the trail in either direction to the creek.

To reach Wakefield Park, exit the Beltway onto Braddock Road going westbound. The park is immediately on your right.

▶ Oatlands Plantation

20850 Oatlands Plantation Lane, Leesburg, VA 20175; (703) 777–3174;
www.oatlands. org

Oatlands Plantation is in a beautiful area out in Loudoun, Virginia, just south of
Leesburg—but it is private, so call and ask about biking details before you come.
Head out I–66 west to exit 67 (Dulles Airport), then take Route 267 (a toll road)
west to Leesburg. Get off at exit 1A, then take the second right (Route 15 south,
Warrenton). Oatlands's front gates are 5 miles ahead on your left.

▶ Riverbend Park

This park is upstream of Great Falls. From I–495, take Route 193 west to Route 603
(Riverbend Road) and turn right. Go 2 miles to Jeffrey Road; turn right onto Jeffrey.
You'll see the main entrance. If you go past the main entrance (on your right), and
then turn right at the end of the road to the alternate park entrance, you'll see the
nature center.

Maryland

▶ Black Hill Regional Park

20930 Lake Ridge Drive, Boyds, MD 20841; visitor center (301) 972-3476

The 1,300-acre park has Little Seneca Lake at its center. Oak and hickory forests
now make their home where mills and gold mining use to be the hub of activity.
There are 4.3 miles of hard-surface trail and over 10 miles of natural-surface trail.
Take I–495 to I–270 north to exit 15B (Little Seneca Lake).

▶ Cabin John Regional Park

7400 Tuckerman Lane, Bethesda, MD 20817; park manager's office (301) 299–4555

This is a very nice park with a small passenger train, an indoor ice-skating rink, and
about 5 miles of trails with several access points throughout the park. It's open sunrise to sunset, year-round. From I–495, take I–270 north to Democracy Boulevard
west.

▶ Cosca Regional Park

11000 Thrift Road, Clinton, MD 20735; general information (301) 868–1397;
TTY (301) 203–6030

Located in Prince William County near Andrews Air Force Base, the park has more
than 690 acres, a lake, an equestrian trail, and a large nature trail network. Most of
the park is undeveloped.

▶ Fairland Regional Park

13950 Old Gunpowder Road, Laurel, MD 20707; general information (301) 699–2407; TTY (301) 699–2544

Fairland boasts 150 acres of parkland along with miles of trails, including nature trails and equestrian trails. The trails extend from Prince George's County into Montgomery County.

▶ Gambrill State Park

c/o Cunningham Falls State Park, 14039 Catoctin Hollow Road, Thurmont, MD 21702; (301) 271–7574

Thirteen miles of wooded trails will allow you to see a wide variety of birds, wildflowers, trees, and shrubs. All trails, except the White Oak Trail, are open for hiking, mountain biking, and horseback riding. Trail guidebooks are available for purchase. All Maryland state forests and parks are trash-free: Please carry out what you carry in. The park is open April through October, 8:00 A.M. to sunset; November through March, 10:00 A.M. to sunset.

▶ Little Bennet Regional Park

23701 Frederick Road, Clarksburg, MD 20871; park manager (301) 972–6581

The park has 3,700 acres of forest that run along Little Bennet Creek. It's only about thirty minutes from the junction of I–495 and I–270.

▶ Patapsco Valley State Park

Extending along 32 miles of the Patapsco River, Patapsco Valley State Park covers 14,000 acres and has around 35 miles of multiuse trails. It's nationally known for its trail opportunities and scenery. All trails on the Avalon Section of the trail system are designated for multiple use except Buzzards Rock Trail, Saw Mill Branch Trail, Valley View Trail, and the trail leading to Cascade Falls. These trails are designated as hiker-only trails. Most of the trails in the McKeldin Section are open for multiple use.

You'll find the park 35 to 45 miles northeast of Washington, D.C. From I–95, take I–195 to the Route 166 exit toward Rolling Road. You can just park and ride.

▶ Schaeffer Farm Trail

Seneca Creek State Park, 11950 Clopper Road, Gaithersburg, MD 20878; (301) 924–2127

Like many of the trails around here, these are multiuse, publicly owned trails. The recently built 4-mile stretch of technical singletrack was built by the Mid Atlantic Off-Road Enthusiasts (MORE). Thanks! The 14-mile trail system includes lots of hills and what is described as a mountain bike "half-pipe." It's a popular mountain biking location. The Farm Trail is connected to Seneca Creek State Park.

Biking Organizations and Group Trips

▶ Bike the Sites

(202) 966–8662; www.bikethesites.com

This firm provides guided tours of Washington and Mount Vernon. Tours take three to five hours, and the fees include bike rental, helmet, water, and a snack. The Capital Sites Tour takes about three hours and starts from the Smithsonian Metro subway exit. Riders should be age nine or older; the ride is considered easy. The Mount Vernon Tour leaves Old Town Alexandria and follows the Potomac down to Mount Vernon. Riders should be age twelve-plus, and the ride is considered moderate.

▶ DC Velo

www.dcvelo.com

DC Velo is the racing team of Washington, D.C. Members have included district champions and past national champions. DC Velo also sponsors bicycle racing in the region. Check out this group to see what racing is all about.

▶ The League of American Bicyclists (LAB)

1612 K Street, NW, Suite 401, Washington, DC 22206; (202) 822–1333; www.bikeleague.org

The LAB is a national cycling advocacy group founded in 1880; the folks here can help you find the name and number of a bicycle instructor near you.

▶ Washington Area Bicyclists Association (WABA)

733 15th Street, NW, Suite 1030, Washington, DC 20005-2112; (202) 628–2500; www.waba.org

The Washington Area Bicyclists Association has information on trails, people to ride with, and advocacy issues; it can also help you with with everything from bike basics to bike parts info. Members receive a newsletter, bike shop discounts, and other benefits.

▶ Mid Atlantic Off Road Enthusiasts (MORE)

P. O. Box 2662, Fairfax, VA 22031; ride information line (703) 502–0359; www.more-mtb.org

Enthusiasts is a pretty good description for the members of this group. They are passionate about mountain biking. They are advocates, builders of trails, and all-around supporters of the sport. They can help get you started or take you places you've never been. Go for a ride with them; you'll have fun.

▶ Potomac Pedalers Touring Club

10366 Democracy Lane, Suite B, Fairfax, VA 22030; www.bikepptc.org

Potomac Pedalers Touring Club is one of the largest and most active clubs in the country. It organizes more than 1,000 weekend group rides (local and regional tours) a year as well as weekday and evening outings.

▶ Virginia Bicycling Federation

P. O. Box 5621, Arlington, VA 22205; www.vabike.org

The Virginia Biking Federation helps to improve accommodation on state roads, highways, and off-road trails.

Area Bike Maps

▶ Washington DC Regional Bicycle Map

ADC The Map People, (703) 750–0510; www.adcmap.com

Available at bike shops or other places ADC maps are sold.

▶ Arlington County Bicycle Map

(703) 228–3699; www.co.arlington.va.us/dpw/planning/bike

▶ Montgomery County Bicycle Map

(240) 777–7200

▶ Maryland State Bicycle Map

(800) 252–8776

▶ Alexandria Bicycle Map

(703) 838–5040

▶ W&OD Trail Map

(703) 729–0596

▶ Capital Crescent Trail Map

(202) 234–4874

▶ Anacostia Tributary Trail System

(301) 699–2407

6 Motorcycle Riding

MOTORCYCLING isn't self-propelled fun, but it is an outdoor activity in and around Washington with a popularity that can't be denied. If you choose to ride, make sure you're as safe as possible. And even if you don't ride, you should definitely check out Rolling Thunder and support the vets.

Rolling Thunder—Ride for Freedom

Rolling Thunder is the largest motorcycle rally in Washington. On Sunday of the Memorial Day weekend at noon, Rolling Thunder departs the Pentagon parking lot for the ride through Washington, D.C., to the Vietnam Veterans Memorial. The Ride for Freedom to Our Nation's Capitol is a demonstration of support for veterans and POWs/MIAs on the solemn grounds of the Lincoln Memorial and Reflecting Pool. It's the single largest memorial gathering in our nation—in 2002 more than 500,000 motorcyclists and their passengers participated, plus another 200,000 in supporters.

Thunder Alley is a colorful festival with vendors from across the United States. There are lots of activities all through the weekend for bikers and supporters. For more information, visit www.rollingthunder1.com.

Safety Courses

Motorcycle riding is not for everyone, but those who ride the open road believe it's a liberating way to commune with nature. Still, this is a dangerous activity that can lead to serious injury or even death. If you choose to be a rider, please take all

Motorcyclists show their support for veterans, POWs, and MIAs during Rolling Thunder.

precautions and go take a class in safety. It's not a good idea to have a friend teach you to ride in a parking lot and then jump right out on the road. Statistics show that more than 90 percent of riders involved in crashes had no formal training—they were self-taught or learned from family and friends.

Many bikers will tell you that most accidents are caused by the other motorists, the car and truck drivers, who don't pay attention to the bikers. They may be right, but more motorcycle training may help in some cases. Whether you want to learn to ride a motorcycle, want a refresher, or just want to learn some safe riding strategies, a safety course is the way to go. A good motorcycle rider training course combines classroom instruction on safe riding tactics with the basics of riding a motorcycle. Courses fill up quickly. Register early.

The Motorcycle Safety Foundation has a helpful referral service that will find beginner or advanced rider courses in your area. Call (800) 833–3995 or (800) 446–9227.

Virginia

Classes are offered at community colleges and other locations throughout the state of Virginia. For more information about enrolling in a rider training class, contact your local DMV customer service center, call (800) 446–9227, or check out the Virginia Department of Motor Vehicles Web site: www.dmv.state.va.us.

Below are some rider training program locations in Virginia:

Blue Ridge Community College, Weyers Cave; (540) 234–9261 or (888) 750–2722, ext. 2304

Germanna Community College (near Fredericksburg), Locust Grove; (540) 727–3008

Lord Fairfax Community College, Winchester; (540) 868–7021

Northern Virginia Community College, Alexandria campus (703) 845–6110; Loudoun campus (703) 450–2551 or (703) 450–2552

Maryland

The Maryland Motor Vehicle Administration (MVA) offers motorcycle rider education courses for new and experienced riders. The curriculum was designed by the Motorcycle Safety Foundation and approved by the MVA. There is both a basic rider course and an experienced rider course. To register or for more information, please call (800) 638–1722 (inside Maryland only) or (410) 508–2436. You can also check out the Maryland Motor Vehicle Administration Web site at mva.state.md.us/.

Below are some Maryland rider training program locations:

Allegany College of Maryland, (800) 638–1722

The Motor Vehicle Administration in Annapolis, Frederick, Glen Burnie, Gaithersburg, Hagerstown, and Waldorf, (800) 638–1722

Carroll Community College, (410) 386–8100

Prince George's Community College, (301) 322–0998

Vets come from across the country to participate in Rolling Thunder.

7 Equestrian Activities

HORSES HAVE LONG CAPTURED THE HEARTS of Americans. They are beasts of burden and beasts of beauty, and racing them has become the sport of kings. But with the invention of the auto came the decline of the horse, and now we must seek out our own connections with horses.

So what do you enjoy? The horses ridden by police through the streets, the polo matches, the horse-racing track, one of the many competitions among riders, or pleasure riding on the weekends? Whether we're spectators or riders, horses bring us back to nature.

Riding and Lessons

There are many places to go riding in the D.C. metro area, and lessons are usually a safe, practical way to learn. You'll need a pair of jeans and a pair of boots with a heel to start. You'll also need a riding helmet—though most places will rent you one. Take some lessons before you start spending a lot of money on riding gear. You may or may not enjoy it. Horses are beautiful creatures, but they are also large and powerful and must be respected. Be patient and pay close attention to your instructors. Find a place that suits your needs. Call and ask about the type of instruction that an establishment can provide. Find out how much it costs for sessions, and whether you lose your money if you miss a session. People have different needs. If you're on a schedule, a planned set of lessons may work better for you. If you're a mom with four kids who works and goes to school, you may want to find a place where you can pay as you go in case you have to miss a few sessions. Find a place where you're comfortable and have fun.

Riding in the D.C. Metro Area

Here in the nation's capital, it's easy to forget how close we are to the heart of Maryland and Virginia hunt country. Both states boast many, many places to ride; any phone book is full of stables that offer riding lessons. In the heart of the city, however, there's really only one place to ride—Rock Creek Park.

▶ Rock Creek Park Horse Center

Military and Glover Streets, NW, 5100 Glover Road, Washington, DC; (202) 362–0117; www.rockcreekhorsecenter.com

For horseback riding and lessons, visit the Horse Center off Military Road.

▶ Loudoun Therapeutic Riding Foundation, Inc.

41793 Tutt Lane, Leesburg, VA 20176; (703) 771–2689 or (703) 771–9653; www.cadcol.com/equitherapy; ltrf@i95.com

A nonprofit tax-exempt corporation providing therapeutic horseback riding lessons to riders with disabilities. Riders are referred by physicians, teachers, and therapists, who recommend guidelines and assess progress. Classes are held at the Morven Park Equestrian Center in Leesburg, Virginia.

Dressage

Dressage is the ballet of the horse world. When performed well, it is truly a sport of beauty. The rider leads the horse through a series of carefully prepared test movements and smooth transitions from a halt through a trot. It shows off the natural grace in the horse and requires a tremendous amount of control, great physical strength of the horse, and a close partnership between animal and rider. The sport dates back to 400 B.C. and is very competitive. Most stables that teach riding either offer some type of dressage or can direct you to local competitions.

The national levels are preliminary, novice, elementary, medium, and advanced. The international levels are Prix St George, Intermediaire I, Intermediaire II, and Grand Prix.

▶ Morven Park & Morven Park International Equestrian Center

41793 Tutt Lane, Leesburg, VA 20176; (703) 777–2890

Morven Park has dressage shows, competitions, and workshops.

▶ Virginia Dressage Association

(540) 347–0363

www.vhsa.com

4047 Ironworks Parkway, Lexington, KY 40511; (606) 258–2472; www.ahsa.org

Endurance Riding

Endurance riding is one of the newest and perhaps the fastest-growing branches of equestrianism. Although organized endurance rides were held in the United States as early as the mid-1800s, the modern sport of endurance riding really began in 1955 with the Tevis Cup, a one-day 100-mile ride from Squaw Valley, Nevada, to Auburn, California. Other rides followed, and the first national endurance riding association, the American Endurance Ride Conference (AERC), was founded in 1972.

Arabs are often thought of as ideal endurance horses, but at any endurance ride you will see representatives of many horse and pony breeds competing successfully.

Endurance riding is now an Olympic event. Distances of 60 or 100 miles are crossed by rider and horse in as short a time as possible. Every 15 or 20 miles, the rider must make a pit stop; here the horse is checked over by vets and must be deemed extremely fit or it will be eliminated from further competition. The 100-mile races must be completed within twenty-four hours; the 60-milers, within twelve hours. Call to ask about the course, as this always changes from year to year. Watch the horses come into a pit stop or veterinary check. Find a good vantage spot for a stream or river crossing. Watching from a few spots is fun, but the finish isn't that eventful—it's usually in the dark. Most events start about 4:00 or 5:00 A.M. and finish around dusk.

Virginia has recently hosted two endurance events:

▶ Cosquine Challenge

Tracy Ingram; (703) 818–4419

This race was last run in 1998. The Cosquine Challenge 100- and 60-mile Equine Endurance Events, put on by the Virginia Trail Conservatory, wind through the Shenandoah Mountains and are some of the toughest courses in the world. The event is held in mid-September, with a 4:30 A.M. start.

▶ Old Dominion 100-Mile Ride

(540) 933–6991

Held in June, this is one of the most respected competitions in the country and is frequently used as training for the Olympics or World Championships. Riders camp overnight with their horses. While each rider only has twenty-four hours to cover 100 miles of rough terrain, the health of the horse is paramount. Spectators may be disappointed at the finish line, because the winners come in at dusk and the rest straggle in throughout the night. The event starts at the 4-H Center in Front Royal at 5:00 A.M.

Steeplechase Races

Races over fences can be either steeplechases or point-to-point races. Point-to-points are often sponsored by local hunt clubs, and you only need some mud boots and jeans to watch. Steeplechases are sanctioned by the National Steeplechase Association and for some reason mean fancy clothes and nice cars. Whichever you prefer, you get to see some amazing horsemanship and can enjoy a tailgate party. Virginia has the best steeplechase races in the world, and more of them—about two dozen—than any other state. There's a race in the Blue Ridge area almost every Saturday from March through November.

Steeplechase Organizations

▶ Virginia Steeplechase Association

P. O. Box 1158, Middleburg, VA 20118; (703) 777–2414; www.vasteeplechase.com

Contact the Virginia Steeplechase Association for a complete listing of the steeplechases in the state.

▶ Maryland Steeplechasing

www.marylandsteeplechasing.org

There are many fine steeplechases in Maryland including the Howard County–Iron Bridge Race Meet, the Marlborough Hunt Races, the My Lady's Manor Steeplechase (which benefits its next-door neighbor, the Ladew Topiary Gardens), the Maryland Grand National, the Maryland Hunt Cup, and the Legacy Steeplechase at Shawan Downs.

▶ National Steeplechase Association (NSA)

400 Fair Hill Drive, Elkton, MD 21921; (410) 392–0700; www.nationalsteeplechase.com

The NSA is the recognized regulatory body of the sport. It's been around for more than a hundred years, with a mission to encourage and advance the sport of steeplechasing in the United States.

Selected Steeplechase Events

▶ *The Virginia Gold Cup Races (spring) and the International Gold Cup Races (fall)*

Great Meadow, The Plains, VA; (540) 347–2612 or (800) 69–RACES; www.great meadow.org or www.vagoldcup.com

The Gold Cup has been around since 1922. Today's version, the largest steeplechase event in the state, has seven races over a 3.5-mile course with twenty post and rail fences. It's a see-and-be-seen event for the who's who of Washington. There are also pony races and Jack Russell terrier races. You should arrive at 10:00 A.M. when the gates open to get a parking place. You'll see some extravagant tailgate parties before the 1:30 P.M. start. All tickets are sold in advance. General-admission parking admits a maximum of six per vehicle. Call for advance tickets and information.

The Virginia Gold Cup Races are held on the first Saturday in May (Kentucky Derby Day); International Gold Cup Races are held on the third Saturday in October.

To get there: Take I–66 west to exit 31, Route 245/The Plains. Drive south for 2.5 miles to Great Meadow.

▶ *Foxfield Races*

Foxfield Race Course, Garth Road, Charlottesville, VA 22905; (804) 293–9501; www.foxfieldraces.com

Yes, this is a hike from D.C., but the Foxfield Races (two major steeplechase meetings each year) are some of the area's biggest events with some of the best riders and about 20,000 spectators. The tailgating has been referred to as right out of the pages of *Town and Country* magazine—a fairly accurate description of the glamour that surrounds the event. There are six races—you'll want to arrive early for some good tailgating. Flat and jumping races start at 1:00 P.M. General-admission and parking fees are charged. Call to purchase advance tickets or to find out ticket office locations in Charlottesville.

The Foxfield Races are held on the last Saturday in April and the last Sunday in September.

To get there: From D.C. take Route 29 south to the 250 Bypass West exit (Lynchburg). Get off at the first exit (Barracks Road—Route 654) and turn right; Foxfield is 4 miles ahead on your left.

▶ *Middleburg Spring Races*

Glenwood Park, Route 626, Middleburg, VA; (540) 687–6545; www.middleburgonline. com/horses.html

Top riders, big purses, and close to 10,000 spectators make the oldest steeplechase in Virginia one of the best races on the circuit. The Middleburg races had their eightieth anniversary in 2000. Gates open at 10:30 A.M. Food is available, but most folks tailgate. Races begin at 2:00 P.M. The price of tickets includes parking. Call for ticket information; advance tickets are cheaper.

The races are usually held the third Saturday in April.

To get there: You'll find the event 1.25 miles north of Middleburg on Foxcroft Road (Route 626).

▶ Middleburg Fall Races

www.vafallraces.com

Middleburg has also hosted the Middleburg Fall Races since 1955. They're usually held the first weekend in October.

▶ Montpelier Hunt Races

Off Route 20, 11407 Constitution Highway, Montpelier Station, VA; (540) 672–0027; www.montpelier.org/races.htm

Historic Montpelier was the home of James Madison until the Du Pont family purchased it in 1900. The family opened the house to the locals for the race back in the 1920s, making this the only public sporting event held at the home of a U.S. president. Proceeds from the races are used to preserve and maintain this historic property. Top horses and riders from across the country compete here at one of the key stops on the National Steeplechase Association circuit. Arrive early and have a tailgating party. Gates open at 9:30 A.M. Jack Russell terrier races usually begin around 10:30 A.M. The first race begins at 12:30 P.M. The main house is open for tours. Call for ticket and parking prices and information. Tickets purchased in advance are cheaper.

It all happens on the first Saturday in November.

To get there: From Washington, D.C. take Route 15/29 south to Culpeper, then Route 15 south to Orange, and Route 20 to Montpelier Station.

Horse Racing

▶ The Preakness Stakes

Pimlico Race Course, Attn: Preakness Tickets, Hayward and Winner Avenues, Baltimore, MD 21215; reservations (410) 542–9400, ext. 4484 or (800) 638–3811; fax (410) 664–6645; www.marylandracing.com

One of the stops on the Triple Crown (the biggest prize in horse racing) is in our own backyard up in Baltimore. The Preakness Stakes is run at the Pimlico Race Course in mid-May. Concourse seating is outdoors but under cover and limited. Call to reserve a seat. The infield is cheaper, and it's also easier to get a ticket. Clubhouse and grandstand tickets are also available; the grandstand is standing room only. Pimlico has a total capacity of about 98,000. After the finish, watch them paint the colors of the winner's silks onto a horse-shaped weather vane atop the Old Clubhouse cupola.

To get there: Take I–95 north to I–695 west to exit 18 and head east to Lochearn (Liberty Road). Go left onto Northern Parkway (seventh light), then right onto Park Heights Avenue and left onto Hayward Avenue. It's about an hour's drive from D.C.

Foxhunting

Virginia hunt country stretches from Loudoun to Albemarle Counties and is some of the most beautiful terrain in the world. The centuries-old sport and accompanying way of life help keep the area from becoming a part of the Washington suburban sprawl. The name of the sport is foxhunting, but don't let that fool you. The modern foxhunt is more about fox chasing. The Masters of Foxhounds Association of America has a no-kill policy. The foxhounds are trained to track the fox, not to kill it. This takes the blood out of the blood sport and leaves the foxhunters with some amazing riding. Some ride fast over gates and across streams; others hold back and bypass the obstacles.

There are more than a dozen historic hunts in the area. They go out several times a week from fall through spring, including holidays. Most hunts last between an hour and a half and three hours. If you want to watch the blessing of the hounds or follow the chase by car, plan ahead.

▶ *The Middleburg Hunt*

(540) 687–6301, ext. 2

This hunt usually meets on the first Saturday in December at the historic Red Fox Tavern in Middleburg and rides down Washington Street (Route 50), hounds and all. The Middleburg Hunt Parade usually begins at 11:00 A.M. Call the Red Fox Tavern for details.

▶ *Casanova Hunt*

P. O. Box 105, Casanova, VA 20139; (540) 371–4749

The Casanova Hunt of Warrenton offers weekend foxhunting clinics for riders.

▶ *The School of Foxhunting*

14605 Lightner Road, Haymarket, VA; (703) 754–3577

The School of Foxhunting gives training to both rider and horse (in case the horse isn't accustomed to riding in a group). The school also leases horses for foxhunts.

20334 Edgewood Farm Lane, Purcellville, VA; (540) 338–6558

JR's Field Hunters also leases horses for hunts. You must pass an evaluation of your riding skills first.

For More Information

The Chronicle of the Horse is a weekly publication that produces an annual hunt roster issue in September. The roster lists race days and secretary numbers for all the hunts in the United States. Call the secretaries for exact times and locations: (540) 687–6341.

Jousting

Jousting is one of the oldest mounted games on record. The earliest incarnations of the sport pitted two riders against each other in mortal combat with lances and armor . . . you've seen the movies. While people no longer try to kill each other, simulated combat at festivals still exists. No more knights in armor, modern-day knights joust in jeans, T-shirts, and baseball caps. Most tournaments take place between May and October. Jousting is often a family sport, jousting skills frequently being passed from one generation to the next—but anyone can learn.

In one modern version, targets are set up and each rider is equipped with a lance (usually about 4 feet long). The aim is to ride at the targets and knock them down with the lance. In probably the most popular version of jousting, called the "ring tournament," the rider carries a long, sharp-tipped lance and attempts to spear a series of three steel rings while riding at full gallop. Rings, hung from three equally spaced arches close to 7 feet above the ground, range in diameter from 1.75 inches down to 0.25 inch. Horse and rider cover a span between 80 and 100 yards. Jousting equipment has never been standardized, and tournament rules vary.

▶ *Maryland Jousting Tournament Association*

www.geocities.com/marylandjousting

▶ *National Jousting Association*

P. O. Box 14, Mount Solon, VA 22843; www.netcrafters.net/jousting/joust/clubs.htm

Maryland

Maryland jousting is *huge*. Maryland was the first state in the country to declare it an official sport, adopting jousting back in 1962. For a full schedule of jousting

tournaments in Maryland, contact www.geocities.com/Marylandjousting/jousting
schedule.html.

▶ The Maryland Renaissance Festival Jousting Arena

Near Annapolis in Crownsville, MD; (800) 296–7304 or (410) 266–7304

What would a celebration of sixteenth-century life be without some armored men
with lances riding around on horses? The point of medieval jousting was to hit your
opponent off his horse with your lance—all for the glory of your king. But if you've
ever been hit square in the chest with a lance when both horses are riding toward
each other at full gallop, you know that it feels as if you've been knocked out of the
county. The wenches act as cheerleaders and bring another dimension of crowd par-
ticipation to the sport. Taunting somehow makes everything more enjoyable. No ex-
ploding lances as in *A Knight's Tale,* but still a lot of fun. The festival also offers a few
jousting rides in which you slide down a rope on a dummy horse and try to lance
some rings—challenging and good for most ages. If you have any problems finding
the rest rooms, just ask one of the nice people walking around in period costume
and talking in Middle English. They're very helpful. The festival involves more than
200 performers and ten stages, including the Jousting Arena. Actors include King
Henry VIII and his royal court. It's all held from the last weekend in August into
October.

To get there: Take Route 50 east to Route 3 north, drive 2 miles to Route 450
east, then continue 6 miles east to Crownsville Road. Turn left and drive 0.5 mile to
the festival.

▶ Calvert County Jousting Tournament

Christ Church, 3100 Broomes Island Road, Port Republic, MD 20676;
(410) 586–0565; www.calvert-county.com/joust.htm

Held annually on the last Saturday in August at high noon (there's also a bazaar and
country supper). The goal is to catch three small rings on your lance while at a full
gallop. There's even a children's competition. Christ Church (built in 1772) has been
host to 134-plus tournaments now and claims to be the oldest continuous sporting
event in the United States—the same claim made by the Natural Chimneys Jousting
Tournament over in Virginia. This one wasn't held during World War II, but who
cares?—they're both great traditions.

To get there: Take Route 4 south to Port Republic, Maryland.

Virginia

While jousting tournaments aren't quite as popular here as they are in neighboring
Maryland, they're still big business. For a complete list of tournaments, contact the
National Jousting Association.

▶ *Natural Chimneys Jousting Tournament (Mount Solon Tournament)*

Natural Chimneys Regional Park, Mount Solon, VA; (540) 350–2510

Held every year since 1821 on the third Saturday in August, this is one of two contests billed as America's oldest continuously held sporting event (see Calvert County Jousting Tournament). Starting out as a competition between two local men to see which would marry a damsel (apparently someone had just read *Ivanhoe*), the event now welcomes riders from Virginia, Maryland, West Virginia, and Pennsylvania. Natural Chimneys Regional Park is also the home of many other jousting tournaments, including the annual Hall of Fame Joust on the third Saturday in June. Admission to the park is $5.00. Come visit the spectacular rock formations; campsites are available. Call for details.

To get there: Take exit 240 off I–81, head west to Bridgewater, and follow the signs.

Polo

Polo, the sport of kings, is the oldest sport in the world. You have to be a good rider to play polo, but anyone can watch—and it makes for an exciting afternoon or evening. Two teams, consisting of four players each, ride at a gallop about the pitch, striking the ball with their mallets. The object is to put the ball between the opponent's goalposts. There are eight periods (called chukkas) lasting seven and a half minutes each, but usually only four or six chukkas are played. Ends are changed after each goal. There are a number of rules—watch a little while and you'll pick them up. Horses are selected for their agility, speed, endurance, and intelligence.

▶ *Potomac Polo Club*

P. O. Box 35, Poolesville, MD 20837-9409; (301) 972–7288; www.gopolo.com; info@gopolo.com

The Potomac Polo Club hosts polo matches on the Mall in Washington, D.C., on Wednesday evening at 5:00 and Saturday afternoon at 1:00 during summer. The polo fields are located next to the new FDR Memorial, between the Lincoln Memorial and the Potomac River. Matches are open to the public, and tailgate parties are a common sight. Dress is usually business casual, but there's no dress code.

The Potomac Polo Club also plays in Poolesville, Maryland, at 18410 Beallsville Road. Check out the Web site for directions, a calendar of matches, and information on learning to play polo at the Potomac Polo School. The club attracts many international players and often holds receptions and parties—many of which benefit charitable organizations.

▶ Middleburg Polo

Kent Field, Middleburg, VA; (703) 777–0775

Kent Field was named for its former owner, the late Jack Kent Cooke. Matches are on Sunday afternoon from mid-June through September. The games begin at 1:00 P.M. Admission is $5.00 per person. Bring along a picnic and tailgate next to the beautiful Goose Creek. Take Route 50 west to Route 624. Turn at the Goose Creek Bridge and watch for the POLO TODAY signs.

▶ Great Meadow Polo

The Plains, VA; (800) 537–3652 or (800) 304–POLO; www.oasiswine.com

Polo is played from June to the first week of September, Friday and Saturday evenings 7:00 to 11:00. Take I–66 west to exit 31 in The Plains. Go left at the exit and continue for 1.5 miles. The Polo Stadium is on your left—enter at Gate 2, POLO GUESTS. Please drive slowly once you're in the vicinity of the polo stadium. The general-admission fee of $20 per vehicle goes toward charity.

For More Information

▶ Polo News

www.polonews.com

▶ US Polo Association

www.uspolo.org

Equestrian Sightings

Mule-Drawn Barges of the C&O Canal

The Chesapeake and Ohio (C&O) Canal stretches from Georgetown to Cumberland, Maryland. In summer you can take a mule-drawn barge ride with costumed National Park Service guides detailing the history through stories and songs as you slip past the restored warehouses and mills of Georgetown or see the locks farther up the canal at Great Falls. Times change throughout the season, but there's almost always a ride Wednesday through Sunday at 11:00 A.M. and 3:00 P.M.—call to confirm times. There is an admission charge. Dawn to dusk. For more on the canal, including a map, see chapter 1, "Trails."

Take a mule-drawn barge ride along the C&O Canal from Georgetown to Great Falls.

▶ Georgetown

C&O Canal Visitor Center, 1057 Thomas Jefferson Street, NW, Washington, DC 20007; (202) 653–5190; www.nps.gov/choh or www.candocanal.org

The *Georgetown* is wheelchair accessible.

▶ Canal Clipper

Great Falls Park, Potomac, MD; (301) 767–3714; www.nps.gov/choh or www.candocanal.org

The *Canal Clipper*—pulled by Nell and Molly—is not wheelchair accessible. Take the Beltway to exit 39, Route 190 (River Road northbound), and continue for 7 miles. The park is located about 12 miles from D.C. at the intersection of Falls Road and MacArthur Boulevard.

The Chincoteague Pony Crossing

The Chincoteague ponies were made famous by the equestrian children's writer Marguerite Henry in her book *Misty of Chincoteague*. How they got to the island is disputed, but they've been on Assateague for about 300 years. Today there's a fence between Virginia and Maryland, which also separates the island's two herds. Each herd is about 120 to 150 animals strong. The National Park Service takes care of the

Maryland herd (northern), while the Virginia herd (southern) is owned by the Chincoteague Volunteer Fire Company.

The Chincoteague pony is a recognized breed. Their salty diet makes them drink and retain more water than other horses and sometimes gives them the appearance of being bloated or fat. The well-being of the ponies is carefully watched. They are rounded up each spring and fall and examined by veterinarians as well as vaccinated, dewormed, and given a hoof trimming.

The Virginia herd must be limited to 150 ponies on the island due to the federal grazing permit issued by the U.S. Fish and Wildlife Service. Failure to keep the herd at the proper size could change the balance of nature on the island via overgrazing, or even lead to starvation. Because of this, the Chincoteague Volunteer Fire Company holds an annual pony auction to find new homes for ponies born on the island.

Pony penning has been going on since the seventeenth century, but the fire company has been doing this as a fund-raiser since 1924. Each year the foals and yearlings are rounded up by the Chincoteague cowboys and swim the channel from Assateague to Chincoteague. The swim and auction are always held on the last Wednesday and Thursday in July. The Chincoteague Pony Crossing has become a huge crowd spectacular. Crowds of several hundred thousand come to see fewer than 200 ponies cross the channel. When I last visited, camera crews had to climb large A-frame ladders in order to see out over the crowd, and the Coast Guard had to create a lane through the many boats there to watch the event. You'll get a better view on television. Other than that, come out and enjoy the festivities. Here's a brief schedule of events:

▶ Pony Swim Day

Chincoteague Chamber of Commerce, P. O. Box 258, Chincoteague, VA 23336; (757) 336–6161; www.chincoteaguechamber.com

Swim Day is held on the last Wednesday in July between 7:00 A.M. and 1:00 P.M. The time isn't exact—it depends on tides, when the ponies are ready, and so on. The ponies swim Assateague Channel at Chincoteague Memorial Park, on the east side of the island. There's no charge to watch, and you can park for free at the high school. The ponies rest in a pen before being herded to the carnival grounds. Come to the carnival (held on South Main Street) to view the ponies and see the attractions. The first colt to come ashore in the pony swim (King or Queen Neptune) will be raffled off at the carnival. You must have a ticket and be present to win.

To get there: Take Route 50 east to Salisbury. Go south on Route 13 to about 8 miles south of Pokomoke City, then turn left onto Route 175 and continue into Chincoteague. To get to the Chincoteague National Refuge, turn left onto Main Street then right onto Maddox Boulevard, which will bring you to the refuge.

▶ Pony Auction

The auction takes place at either the pen or the carnival grounds on the last Thursday in July, 8:00 A.M. to noon. The animals sold are yearlings or younger. In 2000 the average price was about $2,000. Payment can be made via Visa, MasterCard, or cash—no checks. No ponies are sold until a veterinarian clears them. Unweaned foals are not permitted to leave the island following the auction. Transportation home for your new foal must be approved by the pony committee—a horse trailer is usually required.

▶ Swim Back to Assateague

The ponies that are not sold in the auction swim back to Assateague Island the next day, at a time to be announced.

▶ Assateague Island

For more on Assateague Island, see chapter 1, "Trails."

▶ Beebe Ranch

3062 Ridge Road, Chincoteague, VA; (757) 336–6520

Children of all ages familiar with *Misty of Chincoteague* might want to visit the Beebe Ranch while they're in the area.

Spectators greet the Chincoteague ponies after witnessing their annual swim across the Assateague Channel.

More Equestrian Sightings

▶ The Faithful Caisson Horses of Arlington National Cemetery

Arlington National Cemetery, across Memorial Bridge from Lincoln Memorial, Arlington, VA; www.mdw.army.mil

Six horses pull a flag-draped casket on an artillery caisson painted black. It's not an ordinary ride, but rather one filled with solemnity and dignity. They have the honor of carrying a comrade for a last ride to rest in peace with the other honored dead. The section chief, who commands the unit, rides on a separate mount to the left front of the team. The soldiers, dressed in the Army Blue uniform and sitting in McClellan saddles, constantly train for this duty. They are members of the Caisson Platoon of the Third U.S. Infantry Regiment—the Old Guard.

The horses used by the Caisson Platoon are the only official army horses remaining. Four teams of horses make up the caisson: a small team of white Lippizans, a team of white English shires, a team of black English shires, and a team of black Morgans. All the horses were donated.

The casket of any military commissioned officer in the rank of colonel or above (including the U.S. president, as commander in chief) is given a funeral with a caparisoned and riderless, horse. The caparisoned horse is led behind the caisson with the rider's boots reversed in the stirrups: The soldier will never ride again.

Please be respectful when visiting Arlington National Cemetery and keep in mind that a military funeral procession should be held in silence.

There are also two equestrian statues at Arlington National Cemetery. One marks the grave of Sir John Dill of Great Britain; the other, that of General Kearny of the United States. Free admission. Choice of self-guided walking tour or paid shuttle tour (information is available at the visitor center). The cemetery is open daily 8:00 A.M. to 5:00 P.M.; it stays open until 7:00 P.M. from April through September.

▶ Trinity Episcopal Church Annual Stable Tour (the Hunt Country Stable Tour)

Route 50, Upperville, VA; (540) 592–3711; www.middleburgonline.com/stabletour

This self-guided tour—held each Memorial Day weekend—enables you to visit a dozen of the most exclusive equestrian farms and facilities in Virginia. The tour is a generous offering from the farm owners. Participants may change from year to year, but previous farms on the tour have included Paul Mellon's Rokeby Farm as well as Kent Farm, home of the late Redskins owner Jack Kent Cooke. You can purchase tickets from the Trinity Episcopal Church on Route 50 in Upperville, or at any of the estates on the tour. It's held Saturday and Sunday 10:00 A.M. to 5:00 P.M. Tickets are good for both days—and they're cheaper if you get them early. Call for information and ticket prices. Proceeds of the tour go into the church's outreach budget and a program to feed the hungry in Washington, D.C.

To get there: Head west on I–66 for 6 miles to Route 50. Exit west to Winchester. Follow Route 50 for approximately twenty-five minutes to Middleburg. Continue on Route 50 to Upperville.

▶ The Upperville Colt & Horse Show

Route 50, Upperville, VA; (540) 253–5760 or (540) 592–3858; www.upperville.com

The oldest horse show in the country (dating back to 1852) is this weeklong hunter/jumper competition beginning on the first Monday in June. Show events start at 8:00 A.M. and continue until dark. Several thousand spectators visit the show each weekday, and about 10,000 make it to the big show, the Budweiser Grand Prix, on Sunday. Come see some of the finest riding talent in the nation. Admission is charged for adults; it's free for children younger than twelve. Proceeds go to benefit local charities. Call for more details. The show grounds are located on Route 50, 1 mile east of Upperville on the left side of the road.

8 Boating

A LOT GOES ON ALONG the Washington, D.C., waterways. There are sailboats, canoes, outrigger canoes, kayaks, shells (boats for rowing), and canal boats—as well as the many motorized leisure craft, workboats, and cruise ships that use the Potomac and Anacostia Rivers daily. This chapter will introduce you to the many opportunities for boating in the area.

Boating Safety

With all this activity, it's no wonder that safety is on the mind of everyone. You don't need a license to operate a leisure boat, but that doesn't mean you aren't responsible for your actions. A few things to keep in mind:

- Look out for water-skiers.
- Remember that the maximum speed is 6 miles per hour in a no-wake zone.
- Motorized boats must give way to sailboats.
- Watch for the markers—green going out, red right return.

Finally, unless you've grown up on the water around some highly educated boaters or sailors, go take a safety course. Even if you know a lot, you may want to try a refresher course. There's always something new to learn. Learn how to properly pick up people after a waterskiing spill (or in a man-overboard situation), how to navigate a channel, or what constitutes a distress signal. You may never need these skills, but when you do, they could save someone's life. Understanding storms and the weather is always a large part of safety on the water. For marine weather information, check out chapter 13, "Cloud-Watching and Natural Science."

► *The U.S. Coast Guard Auxiliaries*

(800) 336–2628; in Virginia (800) 245–2628; www.uscg.mil

Power and sail courses.

► **National Safe Boating Council**

www.safeboatingcouncil.org

Potomac River Security Zone

Safety isn't the only thing to look out for in D.C. waters. Due to the tragic events of September 11, the U.S. Coast Guard now enforces a security zone on the waters of the Potomac River. The zone extends from the Woodrow Wilson Memorial Bridge upriver to the mouth of Rock Creek (in the vicinity of Roosevelt Island), including tributary waters of the Anacostia River downriver from the Route 50 bridge (New York Avenue bridge).

Please remember that the Coast Guard and the MPDC Harbor Patrol have a job to do and boaters should use every courtesy and respect when dealing with their personnel. Follow all directions of Coast Guard and other law enforcement vessels. Here are the rules as of this writing—but please check with the U.S. Coast Guard for any updates, as these rules may change at any moment.

Vessels or persons wishing to enter the Potomac River Security Zone through the Woodrow Wilson Memorial Drawbridge, including those reentering the zone, may do so between 7:00 A.M. and 7:00 P.M., subject to Coast Guard inspection.

No vessels or persons may enter the Potomac River Security Zone after 7:00 P.M. without prior approval of the Coast Guard captain of the port or his designated representative.

Those commercial passenger vessels within the zone wishing to depart the area or operate after 7:00 P.M. must receive prior approval from the Coast Guard by contacting the USCGC *Albacore* on VFH-FM channels 16 or 22A. (This includes all dinner boats.)

Recreational rowing is allowed on all areas of the Potomac between the hours of 5:30 A.M. and 7:00 P.M., and on areas *upstream of Thompson Boat Center only* at all other times. This means that early-morning rowers should not pass below Thompson Boat Center; if you pass the buoy across from the boathouse, you've gone too far. Also, if your workout will straddle either 5:30 A.M. or 7:00 P.M., please be well aware of your position on the river and ensure that you are not downstream too early or too late in the day.

Sailing

▶ Washington Sailing Marina

Daingerfield Island, 1 Marina Drive, Alexandria, VA; (703) 548–9027; www.guestservices.com

The marina offers sailing and sailboard lessons, boat storage, and yearly slips. It also has a full ship's store and gift shop (Spinnaker 'N Spoke), a galley (Afterdeck Café), and an excellent restaurant (Potowmack Landing Restaurant). Take advantage of the marina's boat rentals, by reservation only, and bike rentals (all-terrain and cruiser models) to ride along the GW Parkway, with panoramic views of the Potomac River and Washington's famed monuments. There's also a launching ramp, so if you own your own sailboat, you can put in here. Call for fees. The marina is located 1.5 miles south of Reagan National Airport on the GW Parkway. It's also home to the Sailing Club of Washington (www.scow.org).

▶ Belle Haven Marina

P. O. Box 7093, Alexandria, VA 22307; (703) 768–0018

The marina offers wet and dry storage, rack storage, moorings, and a launching ramp; it also has sailboats, canoes, and ocean kayaks for rent. From D.C. go south on the GW Parkway and make a left into Belle Haven Marina (the sign is on your right, but you turn left). It's located just south of Old Town Alexandria and minutes off the Beltway. Home to the Mariner Sailing School (www.saildc.com).

▶ Potomac

Jones Point Park, Old Town Alexandria, Alexandria Seaport Foundation, P. O. Box 25036, Alexandria, VA 22313; (703) 549–7078; www.capaccess.org/snt/alexsea/

Sunset sails on the dory boat *Potomac* on Wednesday and Friday at 6:00 P.M. Cruises depart from the T-dock at the bottom of Prince Street. *Potomac* is USCG certified for twenty-eight passengers. Free, but donations are requested. Reservations are required.

▶ The Volvo Ocean Race (formerly The Whitbread Cup)

Baltimore Visitor Information Center, (800) 282-6632; www.volvooceanrace.org or www.volvooceanadventure.org

Where else can you see a fleet of 60-foot sailboats along their punishing circum-navigation of the globe? The former Whitbread Round the World Race comes to Baltimore and Annapolis every four years. The race spans two years and occurs every three. Check out the west side of the Inner Harbor in Baltimore near the Light

These sailors are departing from St. Mary's, Maryland, the end point for the Governor's Cup Yacht Race.

Street Pavilion for team exhibits and information on the Volvo Ocean Race stopover countries. The waterfront festival includes tours of tall ships, live concerts, children's entertainment, and, most important, up-close views of some of the fastest yachts in the world.

Contact the Baltimore Visitor Information Center for information and directions, and check out the Volvo Ocean Race's amazing Web site for information about the race, the teams (e-mail the boats if you want), tactics, rules, weather conditions, and global position reports.

▶ The Governor's Cup Yacht Race

St. Mary's College of Maryland, Teddy Turner Sailing Center, P. O. Box 156, St. Mary's City, MD 20686; (240) 895–3039; www.smcm.edu/athletics/sailing

The Governor's Cup is one of the best regattas in the area. Boats sail from the new capital of Maryland, Annapolis, down to the old one, St. Mary's City. The boats start out on Friday night and sail down the Chesapeake, then up the St. Mary's River. The first winners come in early in the morning and usually can't be seen in the dark, but the majority of boats come across later in the morning or in the early afternoon.

Depending on the wind, you can either view a sea of white from the sails or a sea of colors from the spinnakers. The finish line is between Church Point and Pagan Point on the elbow of the St. Mary's River—a calm spot to moor for the night (many boats raft up here). The celebration afterward at St. Mary's College of Maryland is one of the largest parties on the East Coast—food, drink, and plenty of music. Lots of fun for sailors and spectators. The award ceremony is usually held from 4:00 to 5:00 P.M. on Saturday, leaving Sunday to sail back home. Showers and tender service are available for sailors. The event is held every year on the first weekend in August. For more information or an entry form, contact the Teddy Turner Sailing Center using the phone number or Web site address listed above.

THE *DOVE*

Historic St. Mary's City is also home of the *Dove,* a working replica of a cargo ship that brought the first settlers' supplies to the Maryland colony. The original ship arrived in Maryland on March 25, 1634. The new *Dove* serves as an educational exhibit and traveling historical reminder of Maryland's settlement. You'll find the *Dove* usually moored at St. Mary's College at Church Point.

C&O Canal Boats

▶ *The* Georgetown

C&O Canal Visitor Center, 1057 Thomas Jefferson Street, NW, Washington, DC 20007; (202) 653–5190; www.nps.gov/choh or www.candocanal.org

The Chesapeake and Ohio (C&O) Canal stretches from Georgetown to Cumberland, Maryland. In summer you can take a mule-drawn barge ride with costumed National Park Service guides giving the history through stories and songs as you go past the restored warehouses and mills of Georgetown. Times change throughout the summer, but there are almost always rides Wednesday through Sunday at 11:00 A.M. and 3 P.M.—call to confirm times. The *Georgetown* is wheelchair accessible. There is an admission charge. Dawn to dusk.

▶ Canal Clipper

Great Falls Park, Potomac, MD; (301) 767–3714; www.nps.gov/choh or www.candocanal.org

While both Virginia and Maryland have a park beside the Potomac at Great Falls, Maryland has a big historical house as a visitor center. The Maryland side also links up to the C&O Canal path; you can hike along it or ride your bike down to Washington.

Canal boat rides are offered on the *Canal Clipper* in summertime. Times change throughout the season, but there are almost always rides Wednesday through Sunday at 11:00 A.M. and 3:00 P.M.—call to confirm times. The *Canal Clipper* is not wheelchair accessible. Take the Beltway to exit 39, Route 190 (River Road northbound), and continue for 7 miles. The park is located about 12 miles from D.C. at the intersection of Falls Road and MacArthur Boulevard.

Canoeing and Kayaking

Canoeing and kayaking are simple ways to get out on the river and explore—unlike many other boats, no huge launch is needed. All canoes and kayaks provide an easy entry and a quiet approach if you're nature-watching. Other than the boat, you only need a proper flotation device and a good paddle. Not a lot of accessories required, and it's environmentally friendly.

There are many different kinds of kayaks and canoes—different shapes, sizes, and materials used. In kayaking, you have sea kayaks (more stable design for calmer waters) along with slalom, racing, rodeo, and freestyle models. While a lot of the standard kayaks are still around, many changes in design and materials have occurred over the last ten years. Kayaks have gone from fiberglass to plastic, and smaller boat designs have changed the sport to allow more versatility and even more tricks.

In canoeing, there are whitewater canoes and traditional recreational canoes.

Canoeing and kayaking are great ways to explore the Potomac River and quietly view nature.

Whitewater canoes have extra buoyancy so they don't sink as they fill up with water; there's also no keel, so it's easier to change direction quickly. Recreational canoes are versatile and good for flat bodies of water, gentle streams, or slow-moving rivers. Many people take them camping or use them to explore nature quietly and unobtrusively.

If you want to just glide around and visit nature in calmer waters, try paddling near Georgetown. If you want to see some freestyle kayakers or whitewater canoes, go up to Great Falls and watch them down in Mather Gorge.

Washington, D.C., has some of the best urban whitewater in the world. The Potomac River provides a full range of whitewater, from flat water around the monuments to a class VI drop (class VI is the most dangerous rating for rapids) at Great Falls, just upstream from Washington.

There are plenty of great spots up and down the Potomac for either quiet or challenging experiences. Canoeing and kayaking are sports that should only be undertaken with the guidance of a qualified instructor. Please be smart in your choices and use all the resources available to you, whether they are guidebooks, river gauges, a trip leader, or some other experienced paddler's advice. Most important, use your own judgment based on your experience and skill.

Check out the stream flow and water levels before heading out. Have fun and be safe.

Clubs and Associations

▶ Washington Canoe Club (WCC)

3700 Water Street, NW, Washington, DC 20007; (202) 333–9749; www.wcanoe.org

The Washington Canoe Club is located below Georgetown on the Potomac River. It was founded in 1904 by paddlers from the Potomac Boat Club, which is located 100 yards downstream. WCC has placed athletes on almost every Olympic canoe/kayak team since 1924, when flatwater sprint canoeing was introduced as a demonstration sport.

▶ Monocacy Canoe Club

P. O. Box 1083, Frederick, MD 21702; www.monocacycanoe.org

This friendly Frederick-based canoe club trains members and paddles on many rivers, including the Potomac. Excellent Web site—full of information.

▶ The Canoe Cruisers Association

P. O. Box 15747, Chevy Chase, MD 20825; www.ccadc.org

The Kayak and Canoe Club of Greater Washington holds the CCA Downriver Race Great Falls to Sycamore Island every year in June. The CCA helps with racing and training.

▶ Mid Atlantic Canoe Club

www.holoholo.org/canunews/dcrigger.html

This club has information on Hawaiian outrigger canoe racing (yes, D.C. has outrigger racing!). The club is located in the Washington, D.C., metro area and is an officially registered club with the American Canoe Association.

▶ American Canoe Association

www.aca-paddler.org

▶ Mid-Atlantic Paddlers Association (MAPA)

www.nonprofitpages.com/mapa

From Upstream to Down

▶ Upstream of Harpers Ferry

The North Branch runs from Steyer, Maryland, to Kitzmiller, Maryland, including many runs from class II to class IV.

▶ Harpers Ferry to Point of Rocks

Riverbend Park, 8700 Potomac Hills Street in Great Falls; (703) 759–9018

An hour's drive from Washington, D.C., Harpers Ferry has always been known for kayaking and canoeing, with 13 miles of class I through class III rapids. With staircases and ledges called the Needles and White Horse rapids, you know you're in for some fun. The water is high enough to run all summer (usually April through October).

The waters calm just upstream from Great Falls. The relatively unknown Riverbend Park has 400 acres of forest, meadows, ponds, and streams bordering the Potomac River. Gates are open from 7:00 A.M. to dusk; the gate is locked at closing time. The park and nature center are free. There are also picnic tables and a boat ramp for private launches.

▶ Great Falls

Great Falls Park, Potomac, MD; (301) 767–3714

Great Falls itself is a very dangerous class VI drop—the most dangerous kind of rapids. The first time anyone ran the Great Falls was in 1975. It was done by the team of Tom McEwan, Wick Walker, and Dan Schnurrenberger early one August morning. To this day, they won't divulge who was actually first to go over. Great Falls should only be run by expert kayakers under low river conditions. Kayakers who want to run the falls must speak with state of Maryland officials and sign a release form. Maryland has jurisdiction over the river, while the National Park Service has jurisdiction over the shores and surrounding land. Paddlers can contact the proper officials via the information desk at the Great Falls Maryland Visitor's Center in Great Falls Park.

To get there: Take the Beltway to exit 39 onto Route 190 (River Road northbound) and continue for 7 miles; a road leading left will mark the entrance to the park, which is about 12 miles from Washington.

▶ Below Great Falls

For kayakers looking for fun, the area below Great Falls has class II to III runs. The area upstream from the Old Anglers Inn put-in on the Maryland side of the Potomac is extremely popular for novice and intermediate kayakers and canoeists. People put in both up and down the C&O Canal from this inn. Spectators have easy access to view the fun. If you're at any of the overlooks at Great Falls or Mather Gorge, you can usually look down and see kayakers surfing the rapids.

▶ Little Falls

Little Falls is inside the Beltway above Chain Bridge. It's a short run, but a challenging class IV.

▶ Lower Potomac at Georgetown and Theodore Roosevelt Island

There are lots of spots for flatwater canoeing and kayaking around Georgetown and Theodore Roosevelt Island. Check out "Boathouses/Rowing," later in this chapter, for all the places you can rent canoes or kayaks. Cruise around Theodore Roosevelt Island—much of the back side of the island is not navigable in anything larger than a canoe or kayak.

▶ C&O Canal

30th and Jefferson Streets, NW, Washington, DC; (202) 653–5190

The Chesapeake & Ohio (C&O) Canal stretches from Georgetown to Cumberland, Maryland, running next to the Potomac River and providing calm water for relaxed canoeing and kayaking. Open dawn to dusk. See the "Chesapeake & Ohio Canal Towpath" map and chapter 1, "Trails," for more about the canal, including a map. Also, note that Swains Lock rents canoes; it's on the canal north of Washington, accessible from River Road. Call (301) 299–9006.

▶ Anacostia River

James Creek Marina, 200 V Street, SW, Washington, D.C. 20024; (202) 554–8844; www.jamescreek.com

The Anacostia River within the city is very convenient for some good flatwater

OTHER PLACES TO PADDLE

- New River Gorge in West Virginia.
- Youghiogheny River in Pennsylvania. The upper Yough rapids can reach class IV and V.
- The Cheat River and Gauley River in West Virginia have class IV rapids.
- The Savage River in Maryland has more than 5 miles of white-water.

canoeing or kayaking. From the water, you can visit the Kenilworth Aquatic Gardens or the National Arboretum. The Anacostia River is one of the most beautiful areas of Washington, and the islands are being restored to a natural habitat park.

▶ Belle Haven Marina

Dyke Marsh Refuge, south of Old Town Alexandria, Alexandria, VA; (703) 768–0018

The marina offers canoes and ocean kayaks for rent. You sit on top of the ocean kayaks, so prior kayaking experience is not necessary. Have fun exploring this refuge. Maybe you'll see some loons or a bald eagle. From D.C., go south on the GW Parkway and make a left into Belle Haven Marina (the sign is on the right, but you turn left). It's located just south of Old Town Alexandria and minutes off the Beltway.

Boathouses/Rowing

Boathouses are an interesting part of the boating community. While a few just have canoes and kayaks, most of the boathouses in the area feature sweep rowing and sculling as their central activity. The popularity of rowing has soared in the Washington area, and space for storing shells is at a premium. Many area schools (high school and university) have their own crew teams—you can see their names along the "Painted Wall" in Georgetown. Rowing usually lasts from spring through November. If you've never rowed before, go visit a few of the boathouses and take some lessons. Learning is a growing sense of mastering the craft—stick with it. If you're just not a rower, at least go check out a regatta. Spectators get a lot of pleasure out of the sport as well.

▶ Fletcher's Boat House

4940 Canal Road, NW, Washington, DC 20007; (202) 244–0461; www.fletchersboat house.com; fletchers@fletchersboathouse.com

Fletcher's sits between the scenic C&O Canal National Historical Park and the Potomac River. It's located 2 miles north of Key Bridge and 1 mile south of Chain Bridge, at the intersection of Reservoir Road and Canal Road. You'll know you've reached the entrance to Fletcher's when you see the Abner Cloud House, an old stone building, which is adjacent to the canal. There's a large picnic area located just

A rower enjoys a little solitude on the river near Georgetown.

off the water if you want to stay for a while and watch the water activities. Fletcher's rents canoes, rowboats, and bicycles (you can cruise the C&O towpath). Lots of people come to fish—you can also get a fishing license. Open March through fall. In spring it's open daily 5:30 A.M. to 5:00 P.M.; in summer, weekdays 7:30 A.M. to 7:30 P.M., weekends 5:30 A.M. to 7:30 P.M.

▶ Washington Canoe Club (WCC)

3700 Water Street, NW, Washington, DC 20007; (202) 333–9749; www.wcanoe.org

The Washington Canoe Club (a green building) is located below Georgetown and was founded in 1904. It has placed athletes on almost every Olympic canoe/kayak team since 1924, when flatwater sprint canoeing was introduced as a demonstration sport.

▶ Potomac Boat Club (PBC)

3530 Water Street, NW, Washington, DC 20007; www.rowpbc.net

PBC (a white building with green trim—look for the red ramp with a white star) is located just upstream from Key Bridge in Georgetown. The club offers masters and youth programs in summer and fall for experienced rowers, but it has no formal rowing classes or introductory programs. There are membership fees. No walk-ins.

To get there: From Key Bridge, make a right onto M Street. Continue to Wisconsin

Avenue (this is a major intersection) and make a right. At the bottom of the hill is a four-way stop. Make a right onto Water/K Street and take the road all the way to the end. The Potomac Boat Club is on your left just before you pass under an old bridge arch.

▶ Jack's Boats

2000 K Street, NW, Washington, DC 20007; (202) 337–9642

Located under the Key Bridge in Georgetown, Jack's Boats (a yellow building with a red roof) rents canoes and rowboats. It's a good way to enjoy the afternoon or see the sights. Call for rates. See directions to the Potomac Boat Club, above.

▶ Thompson Boat Center

2900 Virginia Avenue, Washington, DC; (202) 333–4861; www.guestservices.com

Located between the Kennedy Center and Georgetown's Washington Harbor, Thompson Boat Center (a tan building) is a public facility and run by the National Park Service. It rents bikes, canoes, kayaks, and rowing shells/single sculls. Thompson also offers two-day certification classes in single and sweep rowing. After that you can take a boat out on your own. As a rowing coach once said, they're the giant yellow rubber duckies, and people flail all over the river in them. But you have to start somewhere. Many clubs use Thompson as their base. Thompson hosts masters and youth programs during summer and fall for experienced rowers.

To get there: From Key Bridge, make a right onto M Street. Continue to Wisconsin Avenue and make a right. At the bottom of the hill, make a left. At the stoplight, turn right. After this right, follow the road for a few hundred yards until you come to a stoplight. This is Virginia Avenue—make a right turn that takes you into the far left lane. At the next light (just yards after the turn), go straight; this takes you into Thompson's parking lot.

▶ The Swan Boathouse

Washington, DC; (202) 479–2426; www.guestservices.com

Tidal Basin paddleboats are a fun way to enjoy the Jefferson Memorial or cherry blossoms. The Swan Boathouse opens in mid-March and is open seven days a week, weather permitting. Call ahead to check availability and rates. It's located at the Jefferson Memorial on the south bank of the Tidal Basin.

▶ Anacostia Community Rowing Center

1115 O Street, SE, Washington, DC; www.capitalrowing.org

The home of the Capital Rowing Club (nonprofit), which provides novice, intermediate, and competitive programs. In addition, it offers a rowing program for inner-city youths, an outreach program for the visually impaired who'd like to row, and a Seniors Rowing Program for beginners—it's fun but rigorous. Located under the 11th Street bridge next to the Washington Navy Yard. Park in the parking structure at the corner of 10th and O. The best place to view is from Anacostia Park, across the river.

As an added bonus, one of the benefits of rowing out of the Anacostia Community Center is that you can visit the Kenilworth Aquatic Gardens or the National Arboretum. The Anacostia River is one of the most beautiful areas of Washington, and the islands are being restored to a natural habitat park. See chapter 1, "Trails," for more information.

▶ *Alexandria Boat House*

1 Madison Street, Alexandria, VA

The only boathouse in Virginia, the Alexandria (a blue-and-white building) is found about 7 miles downstream from Georgetown.

To get there: The boathouse is located at the end of Madison Street in Old Town Alexandria. From Route 1, turn onto Madison Street heading toward the river. Take Madison Street all the way to the end, at the Potomac. Public parking is available—please do not park in the condo development on your left.

The Alexandria Boat House is just 7 miles downstream from Georgetown.

10450 Van Thompson Road, Fairfax Station, VA 22039; (703) 690–4392;
Sandyrun-fhd@erols.com

Owned and operated by the Northern Virginia Regional Park Authority. For more information about the NVRPA, see nvrpa.org. The Occoquan Reservoir at Sandy Run Regional Park is a public water supply; no swimming or cox tossing is allowed. Parking usually costs around $5.00.

Greater D.C. Crew Clubs

There are many rowing clubs in the area—usually masters programs that can introduce people to rowing. Here are a few.

LOCATION	CREW CLUB	WEB SITE
Washington, D.C.	Water Street Rowing	www.waterstreetrowing.org
	Capital Rowing Clubs—Community Rowing	www.capitalrowing.org
	DC Strokes Rowing Club (This is the Washington, D.C., gay and lesbian rowing team.)	www.dcstrokes.org
	Potomac Boat Club	www.rowpbc.net
	Washington Canoe Club	www.wcanoe.org
Maryland	Annapolis Rowing Club	www.annapolisrowingclub.com
Virginia	Alexandria Community Rowing	www.rowalexandria.org
	Prince William Rowing Club	www.pwrc.org
	Northern Virginia Rowing Club—at Sandy Run Regional Park	Ron Lim; RLLim1@email.msn.com

For More Information

■ Row2K is probably the number one site on the Web for rowing information. It has all the listings for just about every rowing activity you can think of: www.row2k.com.

■ USRowing: www.usrowing.org.

■ Rowers World: www.rowersworld.com.

■ The National Capital Area Scholastic Rowing Association is one of the best places to look for information on local high school regattas: www.nvsra.org.

Dinner Boats/Cruises/Tour Boats

▶ *DC Ducks*

Union Station, 500 Massachusetts Avenue, NE, Washington, DC; (202) 832–9800; www.historictours.com/washington/dcducks.htm

Is it a tour bus or is it a boat? Well . . . actually it's a vintage World War II amphibious vehicle. That's right, DC Ducks has taken these old vehicles and transformed them—giving you one of the best tours of the capital available. It's not only a comprehensive land/sea tour, but also fun. Take out your duck calls and quack at the other tour buses!

Ducks depart hourly from Union Station. The ninety-minute, fully narrated tour covers the Mall, museums, and monuments, splashing down in the Potomac. Guests will enjoy a scenic river cruise winding up at Gravelly Point, underneath the flight path of the landing planes at National Airport. One hour on land and thirty minutes on the water. No reservations are required.

▶ *The* Dandy *and* Nina's Dandy

(703) 683–6076; www.dandydinnerboat.com

Both ships are available for Breakfast at Midnight, Brunch, Lunch, Mid-Day, Dinner-Dance, and Midnight-Dance Cruises. Departing from historic Old Town Alexandria, these boats cruise up the Potomac past the monuments to Georgetown and then back again. These elegant boats are similar to the riverboats of Paris. You can also hang out on the 3,750-square-foot outer deck and check out the stars.

▶ *Odyssey Cruises*

600 Water Street, SW, Washington, DC; (202) 488–6010 or (800) 665–0019; www.odysseycruises.com

Perhaps the most unusual-looking boat on the water, due to its slim lines and glass-atrium dining rooms. Fine food, wine (the wine list has won *Wine Spectator* magazine's Award of Excellence five years running), dancing, live music, and excellent views of the monuments are available on Saturday and Sunday Jazz Brunch cruises, along with weekday lunch, dinner, and moonlight trips. Departs from Gangplank Marina at 6th and Water Streets.

▶ Potomac

Jones Point Park, Old Town Alexandria, Alexandria Seaport Foundation, P. O. Box 25036, Alexandria, VA 22313; (703) 549–7078; www.capaccess.org/snt/alexsea/

Sunsets sails on the dory boat *Potomac* on Wednesday and Friday at 6:00 P.M., departing from the T-dock at the bottom of Prince Street. The *Potomac* is USCG certified

The commuting problem around the Washington metropolitan area will do nothing but get worse in coming years—there doesn't seem to be any debate about that. Local planners are pursuing other avenues to get commuters to their destinations. Another ferry is a distinct possibility. The most likely spot, based upon the highest projected passenger volume, seems to be between Woodbridge and the Navy Yard.

for twenty-eight passengers. Free, but donations are requested. Reservations are required.

▶ *The* Potomac Belle

2412 Belle Haven Meadows Court, Alexandria, VA 22306; (703) 858–5566; www.potomacbelle.com

Custom river cruises on this private charter boat depart from Old Town Alexandria.

▶ Shore Shot/*Georgetown Cruises*

31st and K Streets, NW, Washington, DC; (202) 554–6500; www.shoreshot.com

Located in Georgetown at Washington Harbor. With a ninety-nine-passenger capacity, the *Shore Shot* is the Potomac's fastest cruise boat. The tour is a fifty-minute, 10-mile narrated cruise. Rest rooms are on board, and refreshments are available. Fun for all ages. A great inexpensive way to see all the sights. The boat is also available for charter.

▶ Spirit of Washington *and* Potomac Spirit

Pier 4, 6th and Water Streets, SW, Washington, DC 20024; (202) 484–2320; www.spiritofwashington.com

You can cruise, dine, and dance on the Potomac River aboard the 600-passenger *Spirit of Washington*. This luxury vessel has lunch (two-hour) and sunset (three-hour) cruises. The *Potomac Spirit*, which carries 350 passengers, is D.C.'s only sight-seeing cruise to Mount Vernon.

Ferry

▶ *White's Ferry*

White's Ferry, Inc., 24801 White's Ferry Road, Dickerson, MD 20842; (301) 349–5200

The only regularly operating ferry on the Potomac River, historic White's Ferry has been working the upper Potomac for the last 170 years. Ride the *General Jubal Early* (a fifteen-car ferry boat) across the river when the Beltway is packed or simply as a scenic drive on a summer day. The crossing is between Montgomery County, Maryland, and Loudoun County, Virginia—the only river crossing between the Beltway and Point of Rocks. Hang out at the picnic tables or go to the store and

At White's Ferry you can ride a historic ferry across the Potomac, picnic nearby, and rent a rowboat or canoe and do a little fishing.

rent rowboats or canoes—they have bait for fishing. One-way prices run about $3.00 for cars, $8.00 for trucks, and 50 cents for pedestrians and bicyclists. The ferry operates from 5:00 A.M. to 11:00 P.M. High water or ice could shut it down, but other than that it runs all year long.

To get there: From Maryland, take Route 28 west of Rockville to Route 107 (White's Ferry Road). From Virginia, take Route 15 northeast of Leesburg to Route 655.

9 Aviation

WE HAVE LARGELY LOST our love of travel. The exhilaration the Wright Brothers felt is far removed from our experiences today. We enter a sterile airport with tiled floors and walls, and then board a large bus with wings and tiny windows. The romance is gone. But with small prop planes and gliders, the freedom and thrill return. Learn to fly or just go for a ride. Flying around in a small plane can be a lifetime experience. The beauty of the countryside, the freedom in movement, and darting through the clouds give you the feeling of being one with nature.

Air Shows and Tours

▶ Flying Circus Airshow

Bealeton, VA; (540) 439–8661; www.flyingcircusair.com

Flying Circus holds an air show and offers plane rides every Sunday May through October. It also stages a Hot Air Balloon Festival and air show in August. Always fun to see the "flying farmer."

▶ Capital Helicopter Tours

Washington National Airport General Aviation Terminal, Washington, DC; (703) 417–2150

Hang Gliding and Paragliding

Virginia

There are currently only two launch sites in Virginia, both along the Blue Ridge Parkway. All hang gliders are required to obtain a special permit, available at local ranger offices. A Hang 3 rating is required for both sites due to the steep terrain. A Cliff Launch rating is also required for the Ravens Roost Site. Space is limited, and only two open kites are allowed on each site at any given time. Individual or blanket written permission from landing site landowners is required.

▶ Roanoke Mountain (milepost 120)

East-facing site with a launch elevation of 2,194 feet MSL.

▶ Ravens Roost (milepost 11)

West-facing site with a launch elevation of 3,200 feet MSL.

Maryland

▶ Highland Aerosports

24038 Race Track Road, Ridgely, MD 21660; (410) 634–2700; www.aerosports.net

Highland Aerosports offers instruction in hang gliding as well as tandem introductory flights. It's found not far across Bay Bridge from Washington.

Clubs and Organizations

The best information for launching and flying the area can be found through local clubs and local pilots who are familiar with each site. In other words, don't just show up and expect to fly—get detailed information first.

▶ Eagle Rock Flight Club

flyeaglerock.com

▶ Southwest Virginia Hang Gliding & Paragliding Association

members.cox.net/skywacker

▶ Fly Roanoke

www.flyroanoke.com

▶ The Capital Hang Gliding and Paragliding Association

chgpa.org

The Capital Hang Gliding and Paragliding Association meets on the fourth Wednesday of every month. Meetings are held downstairs at Lasick's Beef House.

▶ **United States Hang Gliding Association (USHGA)**

www.ushga.org

▶ **Wright Brothers' Historical Information**

www.libraries.wright.edu

Soaring/Gliding

Soaring is flying without an engine. The glider or sailplane usually takes off being towed by a cable behind a powered plane. Once at a sustainable altitude, the glider pilot releases the cable and the craft is gliding on its own. The energy of the air currents lifts and sustains the glider aloft. The pilot looks for warm thermals to gain altitude or skirts along the ridges of mountains trying to catch some air. Staying aloft for as long as possible and finding a good soft place to land require strategy and a good knowledge of aviation. The FAA doesn't require a medical exam for soaring/gliding, and you're allowed to solo at age fourteen.

Gliding/soaring presents some unique challenges. At almost any point, you could find yourself without wind. But wind is just one kind of lift. Most of the time gliders soar on thermals, which are generated not by wind but by heat. Some areas of ground (such as pavement or brown fields) heat up faster than water or green fields. Nature says hot air rises, and it does, and so does the glider that finds the thermal—

Gliders wait for a tow into the open sky.

loosely marked by cotton-ball clouds. Part of the challenge of soaring is finding the thermals. A visible "thermal" at ground level is the familiar "dust devil" that most of us have seen.

Many people suffer the misconception that in a glider, you're in danger of having to land immediately if you lose your wind. In reality gliders can glide 20, 30, 40, or even 50 miles forward for each mile down. So if you run out of lift at, say, 2,500 feet, you still have time to look for more lift, while keeping the airport within gliding distance for landing in case you don't. Ninety-nine percent of flights land right back at the airport where they took off—you can't solo until you know how to do that. More experienced pilots who choose to go cross-country know when they leave the field that they may "land out." Here's the tricky part—the number of open spaces is getting smaller each year. In some places, there just aren't any farm fields. Recognize the level of flying you're comfortable with and trained for. Try not to expand your horizons too quickly. Take it slow.

In addition to good thermals, the Appalachian Mountains (which run from Pennsylvania through Maryland, Virginia, West Virginia, and down to Tennessee) have a series of ridges that provide unique updrafts and wave conditions. When the winds blow consistently at more than 5 to 10 knots from the northwest, ridge lift is created. As the winds rise to go over the mountains (windward side), the glider pilot can take advantage of the almost continuously rising air. The winds also create a "bounce" on the leeward side of the mountain, giving much the same effect—long, continuous flights. Indeed, trips of more than 1,000 miles have been flown from the ridge, and altitudes of 12,000 to 14,000 feet are regularly attained. The best soaring conditions are found from March through mid-June and mid-September through mid-December.

▶ Soaring Society of America (SSA)

P.O. Box 2100, Hobbs, NM 88241-2100; (505) 392–1177; www.ssa.org

The Soaring Society of America has the largest soaring Web site in the country—check it out to find clubs in your area or just to grab a calendar. SSA is also the Fédération Aeronautique Internationale (FAI) representative for soaring in the United States. The FAI is the international governing body for all forms of sport aviation.

▶ Mid-Atlantic Soaring Association (M-ASA)

4823 Teen Barnes Road, Frederick, MD 21702; (301) 473–8984; www.m-asa.org

Frederick Municipal Airport, Frederick, MD

Mid-Atlantic Soaring Center, Fairfield, PA (just south of Gettysburg)

M-ASA is a two-site operation that offers primary and advanced instruction, local and cross-country soaring, towing services for owners of private ships, and use of club single- and two-place gliders. It's one of the largest glider clubs in the country and more than fifty years old.

If you want to join the M-ASA, visit or call one of the centers to discuss your interests and determine the best course of action. The Fairfield, Pennsylvania location is sometimes closed due to flight restrictions since 9/11. Call the main contact number above for information before visiting this center. M-ASA operating season starts with a mandatory safety meeting the second Friday in March and extends through the third weekend in November. In addition to fees, time and work are parts of the cost of membership. Since 9/11, the group requires a photocopy of your driver's license and pilot's license (if any) along with your membership application.

The club does not give or sell rides, but club members can take anyone they choose for a ride. You can often get a ride with a member. Just be patient and be prepared to wait several hours. While the season starts on March 15, try to remember that pilots have their flying requirements, too. Some need their Biennial Flight Review (FAA-required) from an instructor. Others must fly with an instructor before flying a club ship or taking passengers (a club safety requirement). You may have a better chance to find a member willing to take you up in late April or May. Nice to know they take their safety seriously.

To get there: To reach M-ASA at the Frederick Municipal Airport from D.C. and points south, take I–270 north to exit 31A (Route 85 north), and bear left onto Route 355—which becomes Market Street. Turn right onto Church Street—which becomes Gas House Pike. Turn right over a low concrete bridge to the water treatment plant and follow the sign to M-ASA.

▶ Skyline Soaring Club

2708 Blue Ridge Terrace, Winchester, VA 22601; skylinesoaring.org

Warren County–Front Royal Airport, Front Royal, VA

Skyline Soaring Club offers introductory rides and instruction for folks at all levels of learning. There is open membership for students, rated pilots, tow pilots, and instructors. Occasionally formal ground schools are taught at Av-Ed (a flight training school in Leesburg) by one of the club instructors.

▶ Blue Ridge Soaring Society

P.O. Box 787, New Castle, VA 24127; (540) 864–5800; www.brss.net

Weekends only. The group is found 25 miles north of Roanoke on Route 311 just outside New Castle.

Becoming a Pilot

You need to be at least sixteen years old, speak English, and pass a basic medical exam. These are the basic requirements for a powered aircraft license. But again, the FAA doesn't require a medical exam for soaring/gliding, and people gliding are allowed to solo at age fourteen. Women are a growing percentage of the pilots out there. Even some Boy Scouts troops include flying as an activity. It's growing by leaps and bounds.

▶ Be a Pilot Foundation

(888) 227–4568; www.beapilot.com

The Be a Pilot Foundation in Washington has a lot of information on how to become a pilot. The group will even give you a certificate for an inexpensive introductory flight lesson at one of its program schools. It also has a database of 1,600 flight schools around the country so you can find a flight school near you.

▶ Aircraft Owners and Pilots Association (AOPA)

www.aopa.org

The AOPA has excellent resources on learning to fly. Check out its Web site and "learn to fly" section.

Airports for Learning

Many D.C.-area airports offer pilot instruction:

▶ Frederick Municipal Airport

Frederick, MD 21701; Frederick Flight Center, Inc., (800) 355–0620

▶ Freeway Airport

Bowie, MD 20721; Freeway Airport, Inc., (301) 390–6424

▶ Front Royal Airport

Front Royal, VA 22630; Cass Aviation, (540) 635–3570

▶ Lee-Annapolis Airport

Edgewater, MD 21037; A&G Aviation, (410) 956–1576

▶ Leesburg Airport

Leesburg, VA 20177; Av-Ed Flight School, (703) 777–9252; Congressional Air Charters, (703) 771–1950

▶ Manassas Airport

Manassas, VA 20110; Manassas Aviation Center, (703) 361–0575; Dulles Aviation, Inc., (888) 8FLY–DAI; Flightech, Inc., (703) 257–9999

▶ Martin State Airport

Baltimore, MD 21220; Phoenix Aviation, (410) 574–3897; Brett Aviation, (410) 391–0210

▶ Montgomery County Airpark

Gaithersburg, MD 20879-4160; Congressional Air Charters, (301) 840–0880

▶ Patuxent River Naval Air Station

Patuxent River, MD 20670; Patuxent River Navy Flying Club, (301) 862–1110

Membership in the Patuxent River Navy Flying Club is open to all active-duty, reserve, and re-tired military members, Civil Air Patrol members, Department of Defense civil servants and contractors, and their immediate families.

▶ Potomac Airfield

Fort Washington, MD 20744; Flying Lemur Inc., (703) 623–9445

▶ Suburban Airport

Laurel, MD 20724; Suburban Flite School, (301) 490–7580; Capitol Air, (301) 490–7580

▶ Warrenton-Fauquier Airport

Midland, VA 22728; Warrenton Fauquier Flight Center, (540) 788–4959

> ## LEARNING TO FLY IN TENSE TIMES
>
> Since 9/11, learning to fly has gotten much harder in the capital area. Expect an identification check. Expect some airports to limit or possibly end their programs if they are too close to Washington. The FAA is limiting the area in which people can fly and pushing the new pilots farther from Washington. These changes are understandable, and it pays to stay abreast of any new guidelines.

Security Alerts

Much like the Potomac River Security Zone (see chapter 8, "Boating"), there have been a number of airspace security measures implemented since 9/11. The prudent course of action is to expect changes to continue and constantly watch for FAA updates. The FAA is trying to balance aircraft operations while countering possible threats to the national capital.

Since we're on the subject of security—if you see anything that looks strange or out of place at one of the local airports, report it immediately to either airport security or the local police.

National Capitol Region

Pilots planning flight operations in the Washington, D.C., metropolitan area should familiarize themselves with all proper FAA security procedures, especially when flying to or from the College Park Airport (CGS), Potomac Airfield (VKX), or Washington Executive/Hyde Field (W32).

Camp David Prohibited Zone (P-40)

The Camp David Prohibited Zone has been changing. At one point, there was a NOTAM (notice to airmen) expanding the temporary flight restrictions surrounding the established P-40 airspace (Camp David) to 10 nautical miles and up to 18,000 feet. Recently another temporary restriction prohibited flights for a 5-nautical-mile radius at and below 12,500 feet MSL from the centerpoint of the charted P-40 prohibited area. Please realize this is a sensitive area. Check with the FAA for up-to-date information: www.faa.gov.

For More Information

▶ Washington Flyer Magazine

1707 L Street, NW, Suite 700, Washington, DC 20036; (202) 331–9393; www.fly2dc.com

▶ *Federal Aviation Administration*

www.faa.gov.

▶ *Falcon Training Systems*

www.falcontrainingsystems.com

Information for glider training.

▶ *The Soaring Safety Foundation*

www.soaringsafety.org

Useful links, FAA publications, and practice tests.

10 Kite Flying

COLORS SPECKLING THE SKY—paper dancing on the wind at the end of a string. Spring and fall are usually the best time to go kite flying, but any windy day will do. The best time to fly most kites is when the wind is between 5 and 25 miles an hour. Any less wind speed and most kites will have problems flying, while if the wind is stronger most kites will lose control. Some kites are better in more wind—most kites today will tell you the optimal wind speed for flying. Check out "Natural Wind Speedometers" in chapter 13, "Cloud-Watching and Natural Science," to determine the current wind speed. Stand with your back to the wind, hold up your kite, and just let the line out. If there's enough wind, it will just climb right up. Make sure you're in a clear, open space—like a field, beach, or park.

Specialty stores have some amazing new trick kites these days, but dollar stores are a surprising place to find good cheap models. Grab an extra roll of string for the truly blustery days—adding tails can help stabilize a kite in heavier winds. Check out your local library and pick up some books on making your own kite. Find a breezy day and some open sky (away from any power lines or traffic) and have fun.

Kite Festivals

▶ The Smithsonian Annual Kite Festival

The Washington Mall; (202) 619–7222 or (202) 357–2700; www.kitefestival.org

Held on the last Saturday in March on the grounds of the Washington Monument. Free. Open to the public. Kite registration is held from 10:00 A.M. to noon on the west side of the Washington Monument. Enjoy special events, workshops, and demos along with competitions in design, performance, and other categories.

To get there: Take the Metro to the festival. The Blue or Orange line will take you to the Federal Triangle or Smithsonian stations.

▶ Kite Day, National Air and Space Museum

7th and Independence, SW, Washington, DC; (202) 786–2108 or (202) 357–2700; www.nasm.si.edu

Kite Day is usually held on the Saturday in the middle of March from 10:00 A.M. to 3:00 P.M. It features kite-building directions, demonstrations, and a chance to explore the science of how kites fly. Free, but tickets are required. Check the Web site for details—search "kite day."

▶ Gunston Hall Kite Festival

Gunston Hall Plantation, Mason Neck, VA 22079; (703) 550–9220; gunstonhall.com

Home of George Mason, the author of the Virginia Declaration of Rights, Gunston Hall holds its annual Kite Festival in March but usually a week earlier than the Smithsonian's. Public hours are 9:30 A.M. to 5:00 P.M. Enjoy kite flying, food, and other fun activities. You might even pick up a history lesson.

Kite Associations

▶ The Maryland Kite Society (MKS)

www.kites.org/mdkites; Marylandkites@hotmail.com

The Maryland Kite Society—organized on January 25, 1969—claims to be the oldest kite club in the continental United States. While its membership hails mainly from the Mid-Atlantic states, MKS also boasts members from across the nation and several foreign countries. The society's many scheduled events include:

■ Fly Maryland at Carrs Mill Park, Howard County. Held the third Sunday of each month.

■ Maryland Kite Retreat. Kite building is featured on Valentine's Day weekend in Calverton, Maryland.

■ Smithsonian Kite Festival in Washington, D.C. See the description above.
  Check out the MKS Web site for more details.

▶ The American Kitefliers Association

P.O. Box 1614, Walla Walla, WA 99362; www.akakite.org

The AKA is a nonprofit organization dedicated to educating the public on the art, history, technology, and practice of building and flying kites.

11 Bird-Watching

BIRD-WATCHING CAN BRING a lifetime of enjoyment and can be done by people of all ages. Whether you're taking nature walks through the woods, mountains, or downtown D.C., you'll find the greater capital region a wonder of bird activity.

Searching out birds in your own backyard is an ideal way to get your feet wet with birding. A bird feeder or birdbath can help attract birds for easy viewing. A good guide such as *Peterson's Guide to Eastern Birds* will help identify those unknown to you. Many people like to keep a logbook of visiting birds near window feeders. A list of the birds and the dates they were seen will soon tell you which birds are local and which are passing through.

When Birds Migrate

The D.C. metropolitan area is part of a great migration corridor for wintering birds. This creates a unique opportunity for bird-watching since many species fly through on their way to warmer climates. Some, like the American bald eagle, will stop and make the Washington area their winter home. Different species migrate at different times. Some, especially birds nesting farther north, leave quite early. Others remain until late in the season. Even within a species, individual

BIRDING EQUIPMENT

A little time, some interest, a good guidebook, and a pair of binoculars are all you need. Surprisingly, a good and attentive set of ears helps out a lot. A discerning ear can help you identify a bird's song without even seeing the bird. Everyone knows what geese sound like, but what about a cardinal, a mourning dove, or the Carolina wren? Not hard if you just pay attention. Before too long you'll be able to tell that a chickadee is in the area without seeing it at all.

birds may leave at different times—often adults will leave before young birds.

Following are lists of birds and the approximate times when they are most likely to be migrating through the Mid-Atlantic area:

July 1–15
- Greater yellowlegs
- Lesser yellowlegs
- Spotted sandpiper
- Bank swallow

September 1–15
- Sharp-shinned hawk
- Cooper's hawk
- Philadelphia vireo
- Ovenbird
- Northern parula warbler
- Connecticut warbler

October 1–15
- White-crowned sparrow
- Marsh wren
- Chipping sparrow
- Common snipe

November 15–30
- Hooded merganser
- American tree sparrow
- Snow bunting

Birds That Stay Through Winter
- American bald eagle
- Black-capped chickadee
- Bluebird
- Carolina wren
- Blue jay
- American robin

Hawk-Watching

Hawk-watching is really fun for those of us who like the powerful birds of prey. Bald eagles winter at Mason Neck, on islands in the Anacostia River; there's even an aerie on the GW Parkway right across from Fort Hunt Park. Another known nesting site is on the Virginia side of Great Falls, above the overlook and best seen from the Maryland side. You'll see bald eagles to the west along I–66 and to the east along Indian Head Highway. Peregrines nest at the Cathedral of the Immaculate Conception in northeast D.C., while kestrels can be seen everywhere. There are many places around the area to watch hawks during their fall migration.

▶ Great Falls

There is an eagles' aerie just upstream from the falls overlook sites. It's on the Virginia side, but can be best seen from the Maryland side. Just up the C&O Canal Towpath from the Great Falls Tavern Visitor Center, look for a path that leads off toward the river. This is probably the best view of the nest, but it will get flooded during high waters and heavy rains. You can still see the nest from the main observation area near the tavern.

Watch a banded osprey in flight.

BIRD GUIDES

Almost everyone's favorite bird guide is *Peterson's Guide to Eastern Birds*—but bird books vary greatly, and many people have different preferences. Check out used-book stores for interesting out-of-print guides. Hawk guides are also good tools—my favorite is *Peterson Field Guides—Hawks* by William S. Clark and Brian K. Wheeler. Considered the best by local bird-watchers is *Birding in the Nation's Capital Area,* second revised edition, by Claudia Wilds.

▶ National Shrine of the Immaculate Conception

After being on the endangered species list for years, peregrine falcons are finally making a comeback—and they've made Washington their home. Peregrines prefer to build their homes on high cliffs, using narrow cracks and crevices to protect their nests. It is no wonder a pair have chosen the Shrine of the Immaculate Conception in northeastern Washington as their home.

▶ Mason Neck

Mason Neck sits off Belmont Bay on the Potomac and is probably the best place around to go bird-watching. The park is best known for its wintering guests, our national symbol, but also serves as home to many other birds and animals, including more than 200 different songbirds, many hawks, ducks, loons, foxes, and deer. Although the wintering eagle population may not be what it once was (due to local duck hunters frightening the birds during their mating season), you can still find some eagles here. Look for them from late November through mid-March. Let the park rangers take you on a walking tour of the park and point out their aeries.

▶ Snickers Gap

A favorite place to see birds of prey during the migration season, Snickers Gap offers views of peregrines, merlins, ospreys, red-tailed hawks, bald eagles, Cooper's hawks, and more. Expert hawk-watchers staff this site every day from September through November. Here are a few of the spot's recent peak days:

- September 20, 1993—4,000 broad-winged hawks.
- September 18, 1998—19,000 raptors—a pretty good day!
- September 18, 1999—4,800.
- September 18, 2000—4,800.

Usually the height of the season is between September 14 and 22, but different birds migrate at different times. The total for the season is usually around 27,000. When I last visited, I saw six bald eagles and one golden eagle. Trying to discern flying birds is much different from seeing a bird perched on your windowsill. But if you hit a good day in mid- to late September, you should be able to pick it up in just an hour or two.

Bring something to eat, a chair, a pair of binoculars, and a hawk or bird guide if you have one. There's almost always a counter from the Audubon Society around. If there's a quiet time without much activity (you don't want to disturb folks in the middle of tracking a golden eagle), ask someone to point out Mickey Mouse or the Capitol Dome or some of the other landmarks. It will make spotting birds much easier when someone says, "There are some sharpies out over Minnie."

To get there: You could just go out Route 7, but the easiest way to get to Snickers Gap from Washington is to take the Dulles Toll Road to the Greenway (also a toll road) going west. Get off the Greenway at the Route 7 West/Leesburg exit. Continue to Route 601, which is at the top of the mountain. The hawk-watching site is the commuter parking lot at the intersection of Routes 7 and 601, 45 miles west of the Capital Beltway (I–495).

Local Bird-Watching

▶ Lake Accotink

Lake Accotink is a good all-around bird-watching spot with many waterbirds, such as the area's great blue heron.

To get there: Exit the Beltway on Braddock Road and drive 1.5 miles east. Turn right onto Backlick Road, which splits and becomes Amherst Avenue. Turn right onto Essex Avenue. Drive down not quite a mile and park near the intersection with Middlesex Avenue. The entrance to the park is marked by a sign that says NO MOTOR VEHICLES. Follow the trail in either direction to the creek.

▶ Riverbend Park

Riverbend Park is also a great place to see waterbirds.

To get there: Riverbend Park is upstream of Great Falls. From I–495, take Route 193 west to Route 603 (Riverbend Road). Turn right onto Route 603 and continue 2 miles to Jeffrey Road; turn right. You will see the main entrance. If you go past the main entrance (on your right), and then turn right at the end of the road to the alternate park entrance, you'll see the nature center.

▶ Kiptopeke State Park, Virginia

3540 Kiptopeke Drive, Cape Charles, VA 23310; (757) 331–2267

Another big migration corridor, Kiptopeke is at the bottom tip of the Delmarva Peninsula. Many birds of prey will fly down to the tip and sometimes stay a little while before flying over the Chesapeake Bay to Virginia Beach. Some weekends are merlin weekends or peregrine weekends; migration times vary according to species.

▶ Mason Neck, Virginia

Also noted earlier in this chapter, under "Hawk-Watching," Mason Neck sits off Belmont Bay on the Potomac. Watch the loons dip under the water and fish, popping up many yards away—sometimes their underwater swims last more than a minute. Or watch overhead for a passing eagle. When the weather gets cold enough for the Potomac to freeze over, you can see eagles and great blue herons fishing the gaps in the ice. Call the nature center to ask about nature walks.

▶ Huntly Meadows

A wonderful place to bird-watch. Take Route 1 to Locklear Boulevard.

▶ Dike Marsh, Belle Haven

Off the GW Parkway south of Old Town Alexandria. The north parking lot has a lot of wading and shorebirds, while marshy areas feature large numbers of warblers.

▶ Theodore Roosevelt Island

Ideal for waterbirds. The parking lot is accessible only from the GW Parkway northbound—before the Key Bridge. See "Theodore Roosevelt Island" map and chapter 1, "Trails," for a map and more information.

▶ Blackwater National Wildlife Refuge, Maryland

2145 Key Wallace Drive, Cambridge, MD 21613; visitor center (410) 228–2677; general information (410) 228–2692

Visitors can tour by car, bike, foot, or wheelchair. The Wildlife Drive winds 5 miles through the marshes and along the Blackwater River. Drivers are permitted to stop at will even though the road is one lane most of the way. Marsh Edge Trail is wheelchair accessible and gives a close-up view of marsh life. Woods Trail is also wheelchair accessible and loops through the woods. The National Wildlife Federation has an annual bird survey here.

To get there: Take Route 50 east over the Bay Bridge, then turn onto Route 16 south just before Cambridge. Turn left onto Route 335 and continue for about 4 miles to the refuge. It's open Monday through Friday 8:00 A.M. to 4:00 P.M., weekends 9:00 A.M. to 5:00 P.M. There's an entrance fee of $3.00 per car.

▶ Caledon Eagle Tours

11617 Caledon Road, King George, VA; (540) 663–3861; www.dcr.state.va.us/parks/caledon.htm

Caledon Natural Area on the Potomac River has hiking trails and a picnic area in a 2,579-acre state park located about 60 miles from D.C.

Bird Clubs and Societies

▶ Northern Virginia Bird Club

P.O. Box 9291, McLean, VA 22102

▶ Maryland Ornithology Society

Cylburn Mansion, 4915 Greenspring Avenue, Baltimore, MD 21209; (800) 823–0050; www.mdbirds.org

▶ Audubon Society

National Audubon Society, Membership Data Center, P.O. Box 52529, Boulder, CO (800) 322-2529; (800) 274–4201; www.audubon.org

By joining the National Audubon Society, you automatically become a member of your local chapter. The society is well known for its bird walks.

12 Stargazing

ASTRONOMY CAN BE A REWARDING PASTIME. Most people enjoy searching for the North Star, Venus, or the Big Dipper. Sometimes we're lucky enough to see a lunar eclipse, or the Perseid meteor showers in August that offer so many shooting stars. With the aid of binoculars or a starter telescope, you can see the craters on the moon, the rings around Saturn, the moons of Jupiter, and all the planets except Pluto. Once you've become familiar with the universe and you'd like to check out a raging yellow dust storm on Mars, though, you're going to have to upgrade telescopes. Check out the Naval Observatory or a planetarium if you want to see more.

Stargazing Sites and Resources

▶ US Naval Observatory

3450 Massachusetts Avenue, NW, Washington, DC; (202) 762–1467

Observatory tours are offered on Monday at 8:30 P.M. Tours include a video presentation, facilities tour, and stargazing (weather permitting). Limited to the first ninety people. The gates open at 8:00 P.M.

▶ The Planetarium at Rock Creek Park

5200 Glover Road, NW, Washington DC; (202) 426–6829

Free planetarium tickets are distributed thirty minutes before each show.

STARGAZING EQUIPMENT

Naked-eye exploration is fine for most people. Learning how to tell the North Star, the Big Dipper, the Little Dipper, and a few other constellations is the beginning point for most astronomers. There are many different types of telescopes and many good ones out there, but it's a wise idea to try exploring the night sky with just your eyes or a pair of binoculars before you spend a lot of money on a telescope. Once you're ready to expand your horizons, you'll find lots of beginner telescopes—it's hard to walk through a thrift store without tripping over one. Hobby shops are good reference points and often have knowledgeable staff. Keep looking up.

▶ The National Air and Space Museum

(202) 357–2700; www.nasm.si.edu

The museum offers a "Monthly Star Lecture" as well as field trips out to Big Meadow State Park to see the stars firsthand. Call for dates and times.

▶ StarGazing with Jack Horkheimer

This award-winning television show (seen on most PBS stations) serves as a fascinating guide to upcoming cosmic activity such as eclipses, comets, meteor showers, and planetary phenomena. You can also check it out at www.odyssey magazine.com, where there's a lot of information for the young astronomer.

▶ National Air and Space Administration (NASA)

www.nasa.gov; NASA's *Mars Global Surveyor* mission www.msss.com; NASA for Kids, www.nasa.gov/kids.html

Meteor Showers

The moon, the sun, the stars . . . the meteors. Wishing on a falling star is fun, and meteor showers can almost guarantee that we'll see a few.

METEOR SHOWER	BEST TIME TO WATCH	PARENT COMET
Lyrids	April 16–21	Thatcher
Perseids	July 23–Aug 22	Swift-Tuttle
Leonids	November 14–20	Tempel Tuttle

Try to find a safe place with an unobstructed view. If you're settling in for a night of meteor searching, grab a lawn chair and some music. Keep warm but don't fall asleep.

To see the stars clearly, you also have to get away from city lights. Too much ambient light will hinder your view of the night sky. In Virginia, head west toward Winchester/Leesburg. In Maryland, head east toward St. Mary's County.

13 Cloud-Watching and Natural Science

TAKE A BREAK on your Outdoor Escape. Lie down in the grass and check out the clouds to see what images you can find—you might be surprised. That one looks like Mickey Mouse. The tall billowing ones look like the Goodyear Tire Man. Those baby clouds over there remind me of the beach. There's no right or wrong. And after a minute or two, the wind shifts and the clouds become something new. Have fun.

Clouds

Here's a brief primer on cloud types for all you weather-watchers:

- *Cumulus.* Small fluffy clouds; they usually mean good weather.
- *Altocumulus.* These clouds look like upside-down herds of sheep. They're higher than cumulus and often come before thunderstorms.
- *Stratus.* A good example of stratus clouds would be fog.
- *Cirrus.* These clouds are reminiscent of long brushstrokes painted high across the sky. They usually mean it'll rain within a day or so.

SAILORS TAKE WARNING

Weather forecasts are incredibly important at sea. A system of warnings has been developed so boaters can better navigate the waterways—and know when to head for shelter.

- **Small craft warning.** One red triangle-shaped flag. Winds up to 38 miles per hour.
- **Gale warning.** Two flags, both red triangles, displayed one over the other. Winds of 38 to 54 miles per hour.
- **Storm warning.** One red square flag with a black square center. Winds of up to 73 miles per hour.
- **Hurricane warning.** Two flags—both red squares with a black square center—displayed one over the other. Winds of better than 74 miles per hour.

- *Cirrocumulus.* These are the high dotted pattern of clouds often referred to as fish scales. If they start moving lower, it could mean wind and rain.
- *Cumulonimbus.* The large upward-billowing clouds often known as thunderheads, cumulonimbus clouds can bring wind, rain, hail, sleet—just about everything.

Weather

Clouds, wind, temperature, weather . . . they all go together. Attention to the weather is critical in many outdoor activities, especially if you're flying or out in a boat. A rapid drop in pressure or temperature may mean a storm is approaching. If you have a barometer on your boat, you should check it every two or three hours. Watch for clouds building up rapidly.

National Oceanic and Atmospheric Administration (NOAA)

The National Weather Service—part of NOAA, which is itself part of the U.S. Commerce Department—is the primary source of weather data, forecasts, and warnings for the United States. Television weathercasters and private meteorology companies prepare their forecasts using this information. For information on NOAA, check out www.noaa.gov.

▶ NOAA Weather Radio

Be prepared for bad weather—buy a NOAA Weather Radio! NOAA Weather Radio broadcasts weather information twenty-four hours a day, seven days a week, direct from the National Weather Service. Prices for these special radios range from $20 to $100, and reliability can vary based on the quality of the radio, the distance you are from the transmitter, and any other outside interference.

The Baltimore-Washington Forecast Office broadcasts over six transmitters:
- *Baltimore (Pikesville), Maryland.* KEC-83 on 162.400 MHz at 1,000 watts.
- *Hagerstown (Clear Springs), Maryland.* WXM-42 on 162.475 MHz at 1,000 watts.
- *Manassas (Independence Hill), Virginia.* KHB-36 on 162.550 MHz at 1,000 watts.
- *Moorefield, West Virginia.* WXM-73 on 162.400 MHz at 500 watts.
- *Frostburg, Maryland.* WXM-43 on 162.425 MHz at 300 watts.
- *Charlottesville, Virginia.* KZZ-28 on 162.450 MHz at 1,000 watts.

▶ Aviation Forecasts

www.awc-kc.noaa.gov/; Aviation Weather Center, www.noaa.gov/aviation.html

Wind direction and speed, pressure, temperature, visibility: All are important when you're flying. Pay attention to the weather forecasts.

channel 16 156.8 MHz VHF FM

channel 22A 157.1 MHz VHF FM

coastal marine zone forecasts by the Baltimore-Washington Forecast Office, http://205. 156.54.206/om/marine/zone/east/lwxmz.htm

The U.S. Coast Guard broadcasts coastal forecasts and storm warnings of interest to the mariner on VHF channel 22A following an initial announcement on VHF channel 16. These forecasts are produced by local National Weather Service forecast offices.

The USCG VHF network provides near-continuous coverage of the coastal U.S., Great Lakes, Hawaii, and populated Alaska coastline. Typical coverage is 20 nautical miles offshore, but can be significantly greater.

Natural Wind Speedometers

How fast is the wind moving? Hard to tell since we can't actually see the wind . . . or is it? Just because we can't see wind doesn't mean we can't see how it affects other things around us. Leaves blow along the ground, trees sway, flags flap . . . all from the energy of the wind. Here are some natural wind speedometers.

WIND SPEED	INDICATORS
1–3 mph	flags are limp; tree branches are still
4–7 mph	flags move slowly; leaves rustle
8–12 mph	flags fly; leaves move; bushes shimmy and shake
13–18 mph	grass moves; small branches shake
19–24 mph	flags flap with much noise; large branches sway
25–31 mph	trees shake and sway; sand and dust fly

Cricket Thermometer

Have some fun with a Cricket Thermometer! Have you ever noticed that crickets chirp faster in summer than they do during winter? Male crickets chirp by rubbing their wings. The warmer the temperature, the faster a cricket will chirp. In cooler weather, his chirps slow down.

Here's how to tell the temperature in Fahrenheit: Using a watch with a second hand, count the number of cricket chirps in a minute. Subtract 40. Divide by 4. Then add 50. This will give you the current temperature in Fahrenheit degrees.

For Celsius, try it this way: Using a watch with a second hand, count the number of cricket chirps in a minute. Divide by 5. Then add 6. This should give you the current temperature in Celsius degrees.

If you have a thermometer, you can work the problem backward and guess the number of cricket chirps you should hear in a minute. It's a fairly accurate thermometer—or at least the temperature will be correct for the location of the cricket.

Punxsutawney Phil

What event is bigger in weather prediction than Groundhog Day? Probably none.

At Gobbler's Knob in the small town of Punxsutawney, Pennsylvania, there lives a groundhog named Phil. Every February 2, Phil comes out of his hole after a long winter's sleep to look for his shadow. If he sees his shadow and goes back into his hole, it means six more weeks of winter. If he doesn't see his shadow (if the day is cloudy and creates no shadows), then Phil takes it as a sign of spring and will stay out.

Shadow = long winter.
No shadow = early spring.

Phil's full name is Punxsutawney Phil, Seer of Seers, Sage of Sages, Prognosticator of Prognosticators, and Weather Prophet Extraordinary. Groundhog Day originates from an old German custom for predicting the weather on Candlemas. Punxsutawney is a rural community in western Pennsylvania, about 80 miles northeast of Pittsburgh and about a four-hour drive from D.C. Phil makes his weather predictions at about 7:25 A.M., so you'll have to get there early if you want to watch. For information, contact (800) 752–PHIL or www.groundhog.org.

14 Ice-Skating

OUTDOOR ICE-SKATING isn't just for states above the Mason-Dixon line. About once every seven or eight years, the Washington, D.C., area gets an arctic blast that lasts at least five days. Temperatures fall below thirty-two degrees for extended periods, freezing over the Reflecting Pool in front of the Lincoln Memorial, the C&O Canal, the Tidal Basin, the Potomac—even the Chesapeake Bay at times. Back in the winter of 1779–1780, the entire upper half of the Chesapeake froze over. People walked from Annapolis to Kent Island pulling sleds of provisions for the islanders.

The National Park Service and local news stations will let people know when and where the ice is thick enough to safely skate. The park service, however, is not responsible for you on the ice. *Skate at your own risk.* The Reflecting Pool in front of the Lincoln Memorial freezes faster than the canals and Tidal Basin, which in turn freeze faster than the Potomac. Once the okay is given, the pickup hockey games and mobs of skaters descend upon the Mall. One problem . . . there's no one around to rent you skates.

So where do you get skates? You can find them at many local indoor ice rinks, ski shops, and sporting goods superstores. There are even a few specialty ice-skating shops in the area. Another quick and cheap place is your local thrift store—you'll often find skates there for just a few dollars. And when's the best time for thrift store ice-skate shopping? Summertime, of course.

Outdoor Ice-Skating Locations

Washington, D.C.

When deemed safe by the National Park Service, you can skate on the Reflecting Pool, the Tidal Basin, and the canals.

▶ Georgetown

Georgetown has had an ice rink down on the waterfront in years past. The traditional location was between the restaurants at Georgetown's Washington Harbor and Thompson Boat Center. Management has had problems keeping the rink open during the winter months because they just haven't had enough skaters. Hopefully it will gather a following and continue on in years to come.

▶ The National Gallery of Art Sculpture Garden Ice Rink

7th Street and Constitution Avenue, NW, Washington, DC; (202) 289–3360 or (202) 289–3361; www.guestservices.com

The old downtown ice rink has been revamped and sits in the new sculpture garden. The once drab, now beautifully landscaped park has meandering walkways taking you past the various sculptures in landscaped gardens. The rink itself has been rebuilt and is surrounded by marble benches. The old building that houses skate rentals, tickets, and lockers has had its interior refurbished and is now flanked by out-

Kids of all ages love skating downtown in the winter.

door patio areas. What is probably the most beautiful new park in D.C. was given to the nation by the Morris and Gwendolyn Cafritz Foundation . . . thanks!

The rink is located on the National Mall next to the National Gallery of Art (www.nga.gov), across from the National Archives. To receive the gallery's free bi-monthly Calendar of Events, call (202) 842–6662, or send your mailing address to calendar@nga.gov. Open mid-November through mid-March, Monday through Thursday 10:00 A.M. to 11:00 P.M., Friday and Saturday 10:00 A.M. to midnight, Sunday 11:00 A.M. to 9:00 P.M. A season pass for the rink will run you about $200. See chapter 18, "The Arts," for more about the sculpture here.

▶ Pershing Park Ice Rink

15th Street and Pennsylvania Avenue, NW, Washington, DC; (202) 737–6938; www.guestservices.com

Pershing Park is only a few blocks over from the National Gallery of Art Ice Rink—if one is full, try the other. It's open mid-October through mid-April, daily 10:00 A.M. to 10:00 P.M. Lessons, sharpening, and skate rentals are also available.

▶ Fort Dupont Ice Rink

3779 Ely Place, SE, Washington, DC; (202) 584–5007

Fort Dupont, one of the old "circle forts" that protected the capital during the Civil War, also has an ice rink, community nature center, and 400 acres where you can enjoy trail walking, tennis, basketball, or softball. The rink hours are extremely limited—it's usually open only for a couple of hours during the middle of the day—but it's extremely cheap to skate here. Open mid-November through March. Call for directions and current hours.

Virginia

▶ Reston Skating Pavilion

(703) 709–6300 (in season); www.restontowncenter.com/skating.htm

Ice Ventures Skate School; (703) 318–7881

This covered rink allows for comfortable skating even during rain or snow showers. They even have five-gallon buckets so the smallest of skaters can have something to hold on to while moving around the rink. Lots of fun for the whole family. Open mid-November through March. Call for details and admission rates.

Ice Ventures Skate School at the Reston Skating Pavilion includes a basic skills program, specialized classes, special events, birthday parties, ice hockey, and broomball.

To get there: From the Beltway (I–495), take the Dulles Toll Road (Route 267 west). Take Reston Parkway north (exit 12). Proceed 0.5 mile and turn left at the light onto New Dominion Parkway. Reston Town Center is on your left.

▶ Loy E. Harris Pavillion

9201 Center Street, Manassas, VA 20110; (703) 361–6165; www.harrispavillion.com

Located on the corner of Center and West Streets in Manassas, Virginia. Open times vary; call for details.

▶ Tavern Square

King and Royal Streets, Alexandria, VA; (703) 838–4200, ext. 214

Ice-skate in Old Town Alexandria at Tavern Square for $3.00 per person for each thirty minutes. Skate rentals are available but limited. Open Thursday and Friday 5:00 to 9:00 P.M., weekends 10:00 A.M. to 9:00 P.M.

▶ Pentagon Row Outdoor Ice-Skating

1101 South Joyce Street, Arlington, VA 22202; (703) 418–6666

Pentagon Row—right next to Pentagon City—recently jumped on the bandwagon to add outdoor ice-skating to its shopping experience. Play, skate, shop.

Maryland

▶ Putt-Putt Golf, Games, and Skating of Rockville, Maryland

130 Rollins Avenue, Rockville, MD 20852; (301) 881–1663; www.rockvilleputtputt.com

Seasonal ice-skating with skate rentals and family passes available. All-day continuous skating sessions.

▶ Herbert Wells Ice Rink

5211 Paint Branch Parkway (formerly Calvert Road), College Park, MD 20740; (301) 277–0654 or (301) 277–3719; TTY (301) 259–4252

This facility includes the rink, a party room, an indoor warming room, and skate rentals. It's open mid-October through March; call for hours and fees.

▶ Tucker Road Ice Rink

1770 Tucker Road, Fort Washington, MD 20744; (301) 248–2508 or (301) 218–6761; TTY (301) 249–4252

Here you'll find a rink, party room, and indoor warming room; lessons and rentals are also available. Open October through March. Call for hours and fees.

▶ Wheaton Regional Ice Rink

11751 Orebaugh Avenue, Wheaton, MD 20902; (301) 649–2250 or (301) 649–3640

Wheaton Regional Park has this covered outdoor rink open from mid-October through March. Skate rentals are available. Call for hours and fees.

Ice-Skating Associations

▶ *The Ice Skating Institute of America*

17120 North Dallas Parkway, Suite 140, Dallas, TX 75248-1187; (972) 735–8800; www.skateisi.com; isi@skateisi.com

▶ *U.S. Figure Skating Association*

20 1st Street, Colorado Springs, CO 80906; (719) 635–5200; www.usfsa.org

▶ *U.S. Speedskating*

P.O. Box 450639, Westlake, OH 44145; (440) 899–0128; www.usspeedskating.org

This is the national governing body for speed skating.

15 Sledding

SLEDDING IS FUN. And yes, it is an Olympic sport (just like curling). The day will come when the snow is high, the schools are closed, and you tell your boss that your car is stuck—you'll want to be ready for some good old-fashioned sledding. You'll need your favorite sled, some paraffin wax from an old half-used candle, and some warm (hopefully waterproof) clothing.

Sleds come in all shapes and sizes. We all have our own preference: the toboggan, the round disk, the classic Flexible Flyer . . . or maybe you're searching for Rosebud. Look around through thrift shops or garage sales for an old Flexible Flyer if you don't have one. The Flexible Flyer Company was sold, and these great sleds are no longer being manufactured.

As kids, my friends and I always sledded in the streets—but then we always had parents at the top and bottom of the hill to stop cars or give a warning. Of course, this didn't save us from the wipeouts that occurred when we were doing the sledding version of aerial dogfights as we tried to wipe out other sleds on the way down, or knock off other sledders. Looking back, it wasn't a very safe activity. Crashing into parked cars or getting run over by other sledders wasn't the best part of the day. My best friend broke his arm when he went down a good slope in the woods and a tree suddenly jumped out in front of him. Find a hill without immovable objects—it's just as much fun. And if you want to sled on someone else's property, ask first. People usually don't mind if you're polite.

Try to remember that there are 45,000 sledding injuries each year requiring emergency treatment. Here are some tips to stay safe:

- *Dress properly.* Wear heavy-duty boots and gloves for extra protection.
- *Inspect your sled.* Make sure your sled is in good condition and working properly.

- *Wear a helmet.* Helmets are commonplace for snowboarders these days—and it only makes sense to don the same protection when heading down a slippery slope.
- *Sit properly on the sled.* Sit up. Face forward. Feet first.
- *Find a safe place.* Avoid streets, driveways, and rocky hills—and stay away from the trees.
- *Learn the correct way to stop a sled.* Crashing into your little brother is *not* the way. (I know; I was the little brother.) Drag your feet or make a sharp right turn.
- *Use your head.* Don't do stupid things. And yes, six people on a sled built for one *is* stupid.
- *Know when to quit.* When you're tired but you think you can make *just one more* run—that's the time to stop.

Now go outside and play!

D.C.-Area Sledding

What's the best place to go sledding in the D.C. area? Find a good hill.

Check out the Washington Memorial. The hill on the Mall isn't bad, either, but the George Washington Memorial in Alexandria (the Masonic Temple) is a much better hill. It's a popular spot.

In Rock Creek Park you have picnic grove 27 on Glover Road and picnic area 22 near Military Road. Also in Rock Creek Park, the hillside below Howard University Law School on Van Ness Street, NW, makes for great wintertime sledding.

For More Information

▶ U.S. Olympic Committee

www.olympic-usa.org

Yep, sledding is an Olympic sport!

▶ U.S. Bobsled and Skeleton Federation

P.O. Box 828, Lake Placid, NY 12946; (518) 523–1842; www.usabobsled.org

The national governing body for the sport of skeleton.

▶ Davenport Skeleton Sleds

www.davenportsleds.ca

Davenport makes sleds for the Olympic sport of skeleton sledding.

▶ Oley Sled Works

www.oleysled.com

Traditional wooden sleds.

▶ Northern Toboggan and Sled

www.ntsled.com

▶ eBay

www.ebay.com

This is a great spot to look for an old Flexible Flyer. You can also check your favorite search engine.

16 Snowboarding and Skiing

Snowboarding

When L.L. Bean starts selling snowboards, you know the sport has gone mainstream. Snowboarding became an Olympic event in 1998—one day some of those punk kids sitting down in the middle of the slopes may be gold-medal winners.

Snowboarding is more difficult to learn than skiing, but easier to master. Knowing how to ski first doesn't help much. Once you fall down the mountain a few times, though, you'll get your balance. After your first day snowboarding, your body learns how to work the board properly; the second day is much easier. When you're just starting out, take a class—you'll get up to speed much faster, you'll get lots of safety tips, it'll help prevent injury, and, most important—you'll have lots of fun. Remember, if you need to sit down (you're injured, you need a break, your bindings need readjustment, whatever), make sure you sit out of the main ski area and in a place where skiers and snowboarders uphill can see you. When you're ready to restart, make sure you look back uphill and give way as you merge back onto the hill.

▶ Eastcoast Boardco

10358 Lee Highway, Fairfax, VA 22030; (703) 352–4600; www.ecboardco.com

The Eastcoast Boardco has been helping Washingtonians get on the slopes since 1988. In addition to helping you with all your surf, skate, and snowboard needs, these folks provide classes at the slopes. They also offer snowboarding trips on various nights of the week and weekends.

Snowboarding Equipment

Snowboards

Snowboards have become lighter and longer. Lighter helps maintain flexibility, and longer can increase speed. Getting a board that's right for you depends on many factors:

- Your height.
- Your weight.
- The type of snow.
- The type of mountain.
- The type of riding you like doing (are you out for speed or tricks?).
- How long you've been riding.

As a general rule you want a board that, when standing on end, reaches to somewhere between your sternum (center of chest) and your nose. The shorter the board, the more maneuverability you have—better for tricks. The longer the board is, the faster. Beginners will probably prefer something with a double kick (the tip comes up on both ends). When you get turned around on one of these boards, you won't do a face plant.

Bindings

Bindings have gotten stiffer and more comfortable. The model of binding depends on your board. The bindings must fit your board's holes; some boards can only take certain models of bindings. Or you can get a custom board and drill your own holes. Your board should come with a list of corresponding binding manufacturers—or you can ask your snowboarding shop.

Bindings can either be step-in or the conventional strap-on models. The strap-on bindings can be used with just about any boot. You have to unstrap your back binding each time you get on the lift, but most have quick releases that make it fast and easy even with heavy gloves.

The step-ins are used with specially designed (and more expensive) boots, so no straps are needed; the boots just click right in. Of course your boots and bindings must be compatible—and surprisingly, manufacturers have not yet created uniform specifications for snap-in bindings. If you want to change boots, you have to make sure they're compatible with your bindings. Step-ins make it easier to snap into and out of your bindings. Rather than having to sit down and unstrap yourself, you just click out. Makes going up small hills and getting on and off the lifts easier. Some say the step-in bindings give you better control over your board, although this really depends on the combination of board, binding, and boot that you choose.

The folks who sell you your bindings should be able to fit them to your board for free. They should also be able to assist you in determining the foot positioning in the binding with which you are most comfortable. Everyone is a little different.

Boots

Boots have gotten lighter and more comfortable. Boards are made for performance—boots are made for comfort. Snowboarding boots are much like any other shoe in that they all fit differently. A Nike running shoe will fit differently than a New Balance—same with snowboarding boots. Go to a shop that knows snowboarding boots rather than just some large megastore. Try on a lot of boots before you purchase. If you're into serious backcountry snowboarding, the specially designed step-in snowboarding moon boots also can "snap in" to snowshoes. No lacing up anywhere.

Leashes

Leashes keep you from losing your board if your bindings come undone. They strap to your leg or boot and to the front binding or board itself. Most resorts require you to have a leash in order to use the lift. No one wants a board dropped on her head from 50 feet! There are straight leashes and coil leashes. Some double as locks that you can use to secure your board when you hit lunch or take a break. Most bindings come with leashes. Use what you have until you figure out what you want.

Wrist Guards

In snowboarding, you end up falling so often that your wrists take a lot of punishment. That's what wrist guards are for—they can prevent pain and even broken bones. On your first day out, it's worth riding with wrist guards. After you get good at boarding, just wear them when you hurt your wrists for extra protection.

Butt Pads

Yep—go get 'em! Okay, they're usually called "impact shorts." Either way, they'll help keep you from bruising your spine, which can happen from falling unexpectedly. You'll fall a lot your first day. It's easy to fall from the back edge of your board coming out of a turn. Impact shorts will protect your back. They're also comfortable and

Lets face facts—the East Coast isn't the best place in the world for snowboarding and skiing. The Swiss Alps, the northern Rockies, and Utah come to mind when we think of great skiing . . . the East Coast isn't high on the list. But if you watch for cheap tickets and lodge deals, you can take a trip around the country for about what it costs to visit a resort around here.

My picks for the best snow spots in the world? Brighton out in Utah is a lot of fun. Jackson Hole in Wyoming is great. And Purgatory and all of Summit County in Colorado are excellent.

add warmth. They go underneath your snow-boarding pants so they won't interfere with your cool mod look.

Kneepads

Always good for when you do a face plant or hit a patch of ice. East Coast resorts have more rocks than we care to admit.

Helmets

Helmets are becoming more of a standard on the mountain, and many places require them. Find one you like and use it. It'll help you ride with more confidence.

Dress for Success

On your first day you'll probably find yourself getting hot, because you'll be working harder than you need to. It's inevitable. Just as in skiing, then, you want to layer up. Snowboarding cloth-ing should be looser than skiwear, however, for more flexibility. Jackets come down in the back to provide protection from the snow. Snow-boarders also need snow pants with a reinforced seat and knees. Snowboarding socks have padding in the back (ski socks have it on the front of the leg). You'll want gloves or mittens with reinforced palms. And remember, when it comes to undergarments, cotton kills.

Snowboarding Locations

Check out the listing of ski resorts later in this chapter for complete information. In the meantime, here are some tips:

■ Massanutten caters to snowboarders, and it blows good snow.

■ Silver Creek is a fun mountain good for intermediate snowboarders—and it's right across the way from Snowshoe.

■ The best deal around may be the season pass good for the combined resorts of Liberty, Whitetail, and Roundtop.

Skiing

Skiing is fun for all ages and abilities. Kids as young as four are sometimes found on the slopes, and many people ski far into their later years. Much like snowboarding, make sure you get proper instruction from a certified ski instructor. The more practice you get, the more fun you'll have. Even experienced skiers should take a class—if you've never had one, you'll never know what you've been missing. You may find a hole in your technique that you never knew about. Refamiliarize yourself with the basics.

Warm up before you start stretching. Make sure you stretch your hamstrings, quads, and back. Skiing is a combination of balance, pressure control, edge control, and steering. You'll use each of these elements while learning the beginning skills—straight running, the wedge, wedge turns, the wedge Christie, and open parallel. And make sure you learn not only how to stop, but also how to get up properly once you've fallen. It will save you so much time and energy. Work on the fundamentals— whether you're a beginner or racing at the highest level, everyone goes through the same basic techniques and body mechanics—from the basic wedge to skate turns for power and control.

SKIING MOGULS

Beginners should generally stay away from the moguls (all the little hills). But if you're learning the moguls, remember that you're not trying to impress anyone, you're out to have fun. *Go slow.* Pick a line, *go slow,* and try to stay in control as much as possible. Learn to ski the ruts, the sides of the mogul, and over the top. Learning moguls will help you pick out other bad habits in your downhill skills, such as overextending or looking down too much.

Downhill Skiing

Downhill skiing has seen many equipment changes in the last few years. Skis have transformed from the familiar straight sticks to shaped or parabolic models. If you haven't skied in a while, rent some parabolic skis—you'll be amazed. These skis have an hourglass shape—they're fatter toward the ends (tips) and tapered close to the bindings. They're also much better at turning, maneuvering, and overall control than you might imagine. It just makes skiing so much easier.

If you're getting geared up for the season, make sure you do an equipment check before you go out. Take your gear to a qualified ski shop and have the staff test your bindings and make sure the boots and skis are up to par. Ski Chalet is one of the better shops in the area that can meet most all your equipment needs.

Cross-Country Skiing

Cross-country skiing is an aerobic, lifetime activity that can be enjoyed even by seniors. Enjoy a day out in natural surroundings as you ski for as long or as short as you like. If you're starting out, go to a cross-country ski area and take a one- or two-hour class. You can try out the rental equipment and enjoy the benefits of professionally groomed trails, well-marked routes, the ski patrol, the lodge, and public bathrooms. Wait until you get some experience before you head out into the isolated woods.

Unfortunately, uninterrupted cross-country skiing is hard to find in the Washington, D.C., area. Chapter 1, "Trails," shows you a number of pathways that support cross-country skiing—but you have only a limited number of days (or even hours) to enjoy them. Either the trails melt or you have to traverse roads that are plowed. Nearby states may have more to offer. West Virginia has some of the nicest areas for cross-country skiing. Herrington Manor State Park in Maryland, White Grass in Canaan Valley in West Virginia, and Canaan Valley Resort at Canaan Valley State Park are some other good destinations. Check out "Local Ski Resorts," later in this chapter, for more cross-country opportunities.

▶ Rock Creek Park

The Rock Creek Golf Course offers a variety of terrain. The park also has paved trails and closed roads, which make convenient ski trails. The 11 miles of horse trails in the park can be challenging. Usually you'll need around 6 inches of snow. Rock

Two cross-country skiers take advantage of the snow by the Mall.

Creek is hard to beat—as good as any place in western Maryland or West Virginia. See "Rock Creek Park" map and chapter 1, "Trails," for more information.

▶ Dolly Sods Wilderness

Monongahela National Forest, West Virginia, Box 1548, Elkins, WV 26241; (304) 636–1800

Administered by the USDA Forest Service, this is one of the best cross-country skiing locations in the D.C. area.

▶ Cross Country Ski Areas Association

259 Bolton Road, Winchester, NH 03470; www.xcski.org

Telemark Skiing

Telemark skiing is a combination between downhill and cross-country. The heel of the boot isn't fixed—just as with cross-country skis—and you have the same maneuverability as with a downhill ski. Basically, then, you get the best of both worlds. Telemarking is difficult, and it takes a great deal of strength, but it also offers a lot more control than downhill skiing while still enabling you to travel cross-country. It's often used by ski patrols.

▶ US Ski and Snowboard Association

1500 Kearns Boulevard, P.O. Box 100, Park City, UT 84060; (435) 649–9090; www.usskiteam.com

Tubing

Tubing has caught on—and in a big way. Years ago we used to take big truck inner tubes and ride them down the hill. Fast and fun. Then tubing became a big recreational sport on rivers; then they were towed behind powerboats. Now all those who don't ski or snowboard can go tubing. Think skiing is too dangerous? Has a knee or ankle injury left you afraid to get on a board? Just really, really uncoordinated? Go tubing!

It's so much fun. Take a tow lift up the hill, then enjoy a long ride down. No skill is involved—you just lie on the tube. There are lanes so people don't run into each other, and they wait for one tuber to get to the bottom before they start the next—so people aren't stacked up on each other. Almost every mountain resort offers tubing these days; some have multiple lifts and runs.

Remember a few things if you're going tubing:

- You're in the snow—it's cold and wet. Dress in layers, with a waterproof outer layer. That includes a good hat or helmet—don't neglect your head.
- You generally need boots, but ski boots are not permitted. You'll ruin the good snow, and you might hit someone with them.
- Most places will allow kids to go tubing, but check with the resort to see if there's an age limit or a height requirement.

Have fun.

NASTAR

The complete opposite of tubing . . . *NASTAR* stands for "National Standard Race," and it's the largest public race program in the world. You can race against your friends or family. And through the handicap system, it doesn't matter how old you are or what your ability level may be.

The U.S. ski team offers promotions through NASTAR. Famous champions such as Daron Rahives, Picabo Street, and Chad Fleischer all started out in NASTAR. It's a natural progression to go to NASTAR and develop some racing skills before moving up. Many resorts offer NASTAR racing; the listings under "Local Ski Resorts," later in this chapter, include this information. If you don't want to race, you should at least go watch a few runs—they're fun and exciting.

The Alpine Responsibility Code

Regardless of how much you enjoy your snow sport, always show courtesy to others and be aware that *there are inherent risks* in all snow recreational activities that common sense and personal awareness can reduce. These risks include rapid changes in weather and surface conditions, collisions with other people, and natural and artificial hazards such as rocks, trees, stumps, bare spots, lift towers, and snowmaking equipment.

Below is a basic Alpine Responsibility Code. Please be aware that every ski resort has adopted a version of the code, often with additions or variations. Make sure you know their rules. Know and observe the code—it's *your* responsibility.

- Know your ability and always stay in control. Be able to stop and avoid other people or objects.
- Take lessons from qualified professional instructors. Learn and progress.
- Do not stop where you are not visible from above or where you may obstruct a trail or run.
- When entering a trail or run, or starting downhill, look uphill and give way to others.

- Always use proper devices to prevent runaway equipment (this usually means using leashes or brakes). Ensure that your equipment is in good condition.
- Avoid people ahead of you—they have the right-of-way.
- Observe all signs and warnings. Keep off closed trails or runs and out of closed areas.
- Before using any lift, you must have the knowledge and ability to get on the lift, ride, and get off the lift safely.
- Do not ski, snowboard, go tubing, ride a chairlift, or undertake any other alpine activity if drugs or alcohol impair your ability.
- If you are involved in a collision or witness an accident, alert the ski patrol, remain at the scene, and identify yourself to the ski patrol.

Local Ski Resorts

▶ *Bryce*

P.O. Box 3, Basye, VA 22810; (800) 821–1444 or (540) 856–2121; fax (540) 856–8567; www.bryceresort.com; bryce@bryceresort.com

Vertical drop: 500 feet

Highest summit: 1,750 feet

Skiable acres: 25

Trails: 8 (3 beginner, 4 intermediate, 1 advanced)

Longest run: 3,500 feet

Lift capacity: 2,500 per hour

Chairlifts: 5 (2 doubles, 3 rope tows)

Night skiing: Yes (Tuesday through Saturday, and Sunday if Monday is a holiday)

NASTAR racing: Yes

Hours from D.C.: 2 hours

Directions from D.C.: Take I–66 west to I–81 south, and get off at exit 273 (Mount Jackson). Turn east (left) onto Route 292 and continue to Route 11. Go south (right) on Route 11 to Route 263, then turn west (right) onto Route 263 and proceed 11 miles to the entrance of Bryce Resort on your right. Follow the road to the stop sign; parking is straight ahead.

▶ *The Homestead*

US Route 220 (Main Street), Hot Springs, VA 24445; (800) 838–1766 or (540) 839–7721; fax (540) 839–7670; www.thehomestead.com; homestead.info@ourclub.com

Vertical drop: 700 feet

Skiable acres: 45

Trails: 10 (3 beginner, 3 intermediate, 4 advanced)

Longest run: 4,200 feet

Lift capacity: 3,000 per hour

Chairlifts: 5 (1 double, 2 tows, 1 J-bar, 1 T-bar)

Night skiing: Yes

Half-pipe: Yes

Terrain park: Yes

Hours from D.C.: 4 hours

Directions from D.C.: Take I–66 west to I–81 south, getting off at exit 240 (Bridgewater). Take Route 257 west to Route 42; Route 42 south to Route 39; Route 39 west to Route 220; and Route 220 south to Hot Springs, Virginia.

▶ Massanutten

P.O. Box 1227, Harrisonburg, VA 22801; (800) 207–MASS or (540) 289–4954; www.massresort.com; snowinfo@massresort.com

Vertical drop: 1,110 feet

Highest summit: 2,925 feet

Skiable acres: 70

Trails: 14

Longest run: 4,100 feet

Lift capacity: 6,350 per hour

Chairlifts: 6 (1 quad, 3 doubles, 1 J-bar, 1 handle tow)

Night skiing: Yes

Snow tubing park: Yes

Terrain park: Yes

NASTAR racing: Yes

Hours from D.C.: 2 hours

Directions from D.C.: Take I–66 west to Route 29 south to Route 33 west at Ruckersville. Go past Elkton for 6 miles to Route 644; the entrance is on your right. Or you can take the Beltway and I–66 west to I–81 south; get off at Harrisonburg, exit 247A. Follow Route 33 east for 10 miles to Route 644. The entrance is on your left.

Notes: Massanutten offers skiing for the handicapped. Call first to set up a class and to tell the staff of your needs. The resort has equipment and instructors able to handle people with a wide range of abilities.

▶ Wintergreen

P.O. Box 706, Wintergreen, VA 22958; (800) 325–2200 or (434) 325–2100; www.wintergreenresort.com

Vertical drop: 1,003 feet

Highest summit: 3,515 feet

Skiable acres: 90

Trails: 20

Longest run: 1.4 miles

Lift capacity: 9,000 per hour

Chairlifts: 5 (1 six-passenger, 1 quad, 2 triples, 1 double, 1 surface)

Night skiing: Yes

Snow tubing park: Yes—2 parks

Half-pipe: Yes

Terrain park: Yes

Hours from D.C.: 3 hours

Directions from D.C.: Follow Route 29 south to I–64 west to exit 107 (Crozet/Route 250). Take Route 250 west to Route 151 south and turn left. Follow Route 151 south 14.2 miles to Route 664. Turn right; Wintergreen is 4.5 miles ahead on Route 664.

▶ Canaan Valley

HC 70, Box 330, Davis, WV 26260; (800) 622–4121 or (304) 866–4121; www.canaanresort.com

Vertical drop: 850 feet

Skiable acres: 80

Trails: 34 (10 beginner, 14 intermediate, 10 advanced)

Longest run: 1.25 miles

Lift capacity: 6,100 per hour

Chairlifts: 3 (1 quad, 2 triples)

Night skiing: Yes (prime-season Friday, Saturday, and Sunday nights and special holiday nights)

Snow tubing park: Yes

Terrain park: Yes

Cross-country: Yes (30 km of trails)

NASTAR racing: Yes

Hours from D.C.: 3.5 hours

Directions from D.C.: Take I–66 west to I–81 south to Strasburg to Route 55 west. In Harman, take Route 32 north to Canaan Valley.

Notes: Outdoor lighted ice-skating rink.

▶ Snowshoe Mountain Resort/Silver Creek

10 Snowshoe Drive, Snowshoe, WV 26209; (877) 441–4386 or (304) 572–1000; www.snowshoemtn.com; info@snowshoemtn.com

Vertical drop: 1,500 feet

Skiable acres: Less than 200

Trails: 57

Longest run: 1.5 miles

Lift capacity: 20,400 per hour

Chairlifts: 14 (2 high-speed quads, 2 fixed quads, 7 triples, 3 surface tows)
Night skiing: Yes
Snow tubing park: Yes
Half-pipe: Yes
Terrain park: Yes
NASTAR racing: Yes
Hours from D.C.: 6 hours
Directions from D.C.: Take I–66 west to I–81. In Harrisonburg, Virginia, take Route 33 west into Franklin, then head south on Route 220 to Vanderpool. Take Route 84 west to Frost, then Routes 92/28 north to New Route 66 to Cass. Continue on to Snowshoe.

▶ Timberline

488 Timberline Road, Canaan Valley, WV 26260; (800) SNOWING or (304) 866–4801; www.timberlineresort.com

Vertical drop: 1,000 feet
Highest summit: 4,268 feet
Annual snowfall: 150 inches
Skiable acres: 91
Trails: 35 (16 beginner, 10 intermediate, 9 advanced)
Longest run: 2 miles
Lift capacity: 4,000 per hour
Chairlifts: 3 (1 triple, 2 doubles)
Night skiing: Yes
Half-pipe: Yes
Terrain park: Yes—2 parks
Cross-country: Yes (17 km of trails)
NASTAR racing: Yes
Hours from D.C.: 4 hours
Directions from D.C.: Take I–66 west to Route 55 west. In Strasburg, Virginia, follow Route 55 west to Route 32 north at Harman, then follow Route 32 north to Canaan Valley.

▶ Winterplace

P.O. Box 1, Flat Top, WV 25841; (800) 607–SNOW or (304) 787–3221; fax (304) 787–9885; snow report line (800) 258–3127; www.winterplace.com; winterplace@winterplace.com

Vertical drop: 603 feet
Highest summit: 3,600 feet
Skiable acres: 90-plus
Trails: 27 (11 beginner, 12 intermediate, 4 advanced)

Longest run: 1.25 miles

Lift capacity: 13,000 per hour

Chairlifts: 9 (2 quads, 3 triples, 2 doubles, 2 surface)

Night skiing: Yes (25 slopes plus snowboard park)

Snow tubing park: Yes (16 lanes, 5 lifts)

Half-pipe: Yes

Terrain park: Yes

Hours from D.C.: 5 hours

Directions from D.C.: Located just two minutes off I–77, exit 28 (Ghent/Flat Top, West Virginia). Halfway between Princeton and Beckley, West Virginia.

Notes: Largest snow tubing park in West Virginia. To preorder lift tickets call Express Ski at (800) 977–3754.

▶ Wisp

P.O. Box 629, 296 Marsh Hill Road, McHenry, MD 21541; (301) 387–4911; fax (301) 387–4797; www.skiwisp.com; wispinfo@gcnet.net

Vertical drop: 610 feet

Highest summit: 3,080 feet

Annual snowfall: 93 inches

Skiable acres: 80

Trails: 22

Longest run: 1.5 miles

Lift capacity: 9,120 per hour

Chairlifts: 7 (2 triples, 3 doubles, 1 rope tow, 1 handle tow)

Night skiing: Yes

Snow tubing park: Yes

Half-pipe: Yes

Terrain park: Yes

Hours from D.C.: Less than 3 hours

Directions from D.C.: From the Beltway (I–495), take I–270 north to I–70 west toward Hancock, Maryland. Then take the left exit for I–68 west to Cumberland, Maryland. Stay on I–68 through Cumberland and look for exit 14A (Route 219 south). Follow Route 219 for about 16 miles into McHenry and follow signs to Wisp.

▶ Alpine Mountain

P.O. Box 309, Route 447, Analomink, PA 18320; (570) 595–2150; fax (570) 424–0310; www.alpinemountain.com; alpinemt@ptd.net

Vertical drop: 500 feet

Skiable acres: Less than 60

Trails: 21 (3 beginner, 12 intermediate, 6 advanced)

Longest run: 3,500 feet

Lift capacity: 5,800 per hour

Chairlifts: 3 (2 quads, 1 double)

Night skiing: Yes

Snow tubing park: Yes

Half-pipe: Yes

Terrain park: Yes

Hours from D.C.: 4 hours

Directions from D.C.: Take I–95 north past Philadelphia. Take I–80 to exit 52. Follow Route 447 north. The resort is 5 miles past the town of Analomink, Pennsylvania.

▶ Bear Creek

101 Doe Mountain Lane, Macungie, PA 18062; (800) 682–7107 or (610) 682–7100; www.skibearcreek.com; skibearcreek@skibearcreek.com

Vertical drop: 510 feet

Highest summit: 1,100 feet

Skiable acres: 86

Trails: 17 (6 beginner, 6 intermediate, 3 advanced)

Longest run: 7,400 feet

Lift capacity: 7,000 per hour

Chairlifts: 7 (1 triple, 3 doubles, 1 T-bar, 2 rope tows)

Night skiing: Yes (17 trails)

Snow tubing park: Yes

Half-pipe: Yes

Terrain park: Yes

NASTAR racing: Yes

Hours from D.C.: 3 hours

Directions from D.C.: Take I–95 north to Route 202 north, to Route 100 north to Hareford (approximately 55 miles). Take a left at the traffic light at the Route 29 intersection (at Turkey Hill Market). Continue 4 miles to Bear Creek.

▶ Big Boulder/Jack Frost

P.O. Box 702, Blakeslee, PA 18610; (800) 468–2442; snow report line (800) 475–SNOW; www.big2resorts.com or www.bbjf.com

Vertical drop: Big Boulder, 475 feet; Jack Frost, 600 feet

Skiable acres: Less than 130 combined

Trails: Big Boulder, 14 (4 beginner, 5 intermediate, 5 advanced); Jack Frost, 25 (4 beginner, 9 intermediate, 10 advanced, 2 expert)

Longest run: Big Boulder, 2,900 feet; Jack Frost, 3,200 feet

Lift capacity: Big Boulder, 9,600 per hour; Jack Frost, 11,000 per hour

Chairlifts: Big Boulder, 7 (2 triples, 5 doubles); Jack Frost, 9 (1 quad, 2 triples, 4 doubles)

Night skiing: Big Boulder only

Snow tubing park: Yes (both areas)

Half-pipe: Yes (both areas)

Terrain park: Yes (both areas)

Hours from D.C.: 4 hours

Directions from D.C.: To reach Big Boulder from Pocono exit 35 off I–476 (the northeast extension of the Pennsylvania Turnpike), follow signs to I–80 and take I–80 east to PA exit 43. Turn right onto Route 115 south, then turn right onto Route 903 south and follow the signs to Big Boulder. To reach Jack Frost from Pocono exit 35 off I–476, take Route 940 east and follow signs 4 miles to the ski area entrance on your left.

▶ Knob

P.O. Box 247, Claysburg, PA 16625; (800) 458–3403 or (814) 239–511; www.blueknob.com

Vertical drop: 1,072 feet

Highest summit: 3,172 feet

Annual snowfall: Less than 100 inches

Skiable acres: 100

Trails: 34 (6 beginner, 14 intermediate, 14 advanced)

Longest run: 2 miles

Lift capacity: 5,200 per hour

Chairlifts: 6 (2 triples, 2 doubles, 2 surface)

Night skiing: Yes

Snow tubing park: Yes

Terrain park: Yes

NASTAR racing: Yes

Hours from D.C.: 2 hours

Directions from D.C.: From exit 11 (Bedford) off the Pennsylvania Turnpike, take I–99 (Route 220) north to Osterburg, then Route 869 west to Pavia. From I–80 or Route 22 east, take I–99 (Route 220) south to East Freedom, then Route 164 east through Portage.

▶ Blue Mountain

P.O. Box 216, Palmerton, PA 18071; (610) 826–7700; fax (610) 826–7828; www.skibluemt.com; information@skibluemt.com

Vertical drop: 1,082 feet

Skiable acres: 75

Trails: 27

Longest run: 6,400 feet

Lift capacity: 8,400 per hour

Chairlifts: 8 (1 high-speed quad, 4 doubles, 1 T-bar, 2 surface lifts)

Night skiing: Yes

Snow tubing park: Yes

Half-pipe: Yes

Terrain park: Yes

Hours from D.C.: 4 hours

Directions from D.C.: From Baltimore (165 miles), take Route 83 north to Harrisburg, then take I–81 north to I–78 east. Take exit 15 (Route 22 east) to Whitehall. Then take Route 145 north (MacArthur Road) about 9 miles to the traffic light at the far end of a long bridge. Turn right onto Blue Mountain Drive, and go straight through Cherryville to Danielsville, then through Danielsville. Look for the entrance sign just past the top of the mountain.

▶ Camelback

P.O. Box 168, Tannersville, PA 18372; (570) 629–1661; fax (570) 620–0942; snow report line (800) 233–8100; www.skicamelback.com; sales@skicamelback.com

Vertical drop: 800 feet

Annual snowfall: 50 inches

Skiable acres: 156

Trails: 33

Longest run: 1 mile

Lift capacity: 18,600 per hour

Chairlifts: 13 (including 2 high-speed quads)

Night skiing: Yes

Snow tubing park: Yes

Half-pipe: Yes

Terrain park: Yes

NASTAR racing: Yes

Hours from D.C.: 4.5 hours

Directions from D.C.: Take I–95 north to Philadelphia, then I-476 (the northeast extension of the Pennsylvania Turnpike) heading north to Lehigh Valley. Take exit 56 (old exit 33) onto Route 22 east. Continue to Route 33 north to I-80 west, and take exit 299 (old exit 45) in Tannersville. Then follow the signs for Camelback.

▶ Ski Denton

P.O. Box 367, Coudersport, PA 16915; (814) 435–2115; www.skidenton.com; skidentn@penn.com

Vertical drop: 650 feet

Skiable acres: 75

Trails: 20 (7 beginner, 6 intermediate, 7 advanced)

Longest run: 1 mile

Lift capacity: 4,200 per hour

Chairlifts: 5 (1 triple, 1 double, 2 poma lifts, 1 handle tow)

Night skiing: Yes

Snow tubing park: Yes

Terrain park: Yes

Hours from D.C.: 6.5 hours

Directions from D.C.: Take I–95 north to Harrisburg. From Harrisburg, continue north on Route 15 to Route 6 west at Mansfield.

▶ Elk Mountain

RR 2, Box 3328, Union Dale, PA 18470-9528; (570) 679–4400; snow report line (800) 233–4131; www.elkskier.com; elkskier@nep.net

Vertical drop: 1,000 feet

Skiable acres: 235

Trails: 27 (6 beginner, 10 intermediate, 11 advanced)

Longest run: 1.75 miles

Lift capacity: 5,400 per hour

Chairlifts: 6 (1 quad, 5 doubles)

Night skiing: Yes

Terrain park: Yes

Hours from D.C.: 5 hours

Directions from D.C.: Take I–81 north to exit 63 to Route 374 east.

▶ Hidden Valley

1 Craighead Drive, Hidden Valley, PA 15502; (800) 458–0175 or (814) 443–8000; snow report line (800) 433–SKII; www.hiddenvalleyresort.com

Vertical drop: 610 feet

Highest summit: 2,900 feet

Annual snowfall: Less than 120 inches

Skiable acres: Less than 100

Trails: 25 (7 beginner, 13 intermediate, 5 advanced)

Longest run: 1 mile

Lift capacity: 12,000 per hour

Chairlifts: 8 (1 quad, 2 triples, 3 doubles, 2 pony tows)

Night skiing: Yes

Snow tubing park: Yes

Half-pipe: Yes

Terrain park: Yes

Cross-country: Yes (30 miles of trails)

Hours from D.C.: 3 hours

Directions from D.C.: Take I–95 to I–270, to I–70, to I–76 (the Pennsylvania

Turnpike). Take the turnpike to exit 10 (Somerset), then head west on Route 31 for 10 miles to Hidden Valley Resort.

▶ Laurel Mountain

P.O. Box 657, Ligonier, PA 15658; (877) 754–5287 or (724) 238–9860; www.skilaurelmountain.com; info@skilaurelmountain.com

Vertical drop: 900 feet

Highest summit: 2,800 feet

Skiable acres: 70

Trails: 20 (10 beginner, 6 intermediate, 3 advanced, 1 expert)

Lift capacity: 3,600 per hour

Chairlifts: 5 (1 quad, 1 double, 3 handle tows)

Night skiing: Yes

Snow tubing park: Yes

Half-pipe: Yes

Terrain park: Yes

Hours from D.C.: 3 hours

Directions from D.C.: Take I–495 (the Beltway) to I–270 north, to I–70 north, to the Pennsylvania Turnpike heading west. Continue to exit 10 (Somerset). Turn left at the light onto Route 601 north. Route 601 becomes Route 985 north. Follow 985 north to Route 30 west in Jennerstown. At the light, turn left onto Route 30 west. Travel approximately 5 miles to the top of Laurel Mountain. Make a left onto Summit Road (look for the sign). Follow Summit Road for approximately 2 miles to Laurel Mountain Ski Resort.

Notes: Closed down in 1989, reopened in 1998 with a lot of improvements; check the Web site for details.

▶ Liberty Mountain

P.O. Box SKI, Carroll Valley, PA 17320; (717) 642–8282; fax (717) 642–6534; snow report line (717) 642–9000; www.skiliberty.com; skiliberty@skiliberty.com

Vertical drop: 600 feet

Skiable acres: 100

Trails: 16

Longest run: 5,200 feet

Lift capacity: 10,920 per hour

Chairlifts: 8 (3 quads, 3 doubles, 1 J-bar, 1 children's handle tow)

Night skiing: Yes

Snow tubing park: Yes

Half-pipe: Yes

Terrain park: Yes

NASTAR racing: Yes

Hours from D.C.: 1 hour

Directions from D.C.: Take I–270 north to Frederick, then take Route 15 north to Emmitsburg, Maryland, exiting onto South Seton Avenue. At the traffic light, turn left onto Route 140. At the Pennsylvania line, Route 140 becomes Route 16. Turn right onto Route 16; Ski Liberty is 3 miles on your right.

Notes: Ski Liberty, Ski Roundtop, Ski Windham, and Whitetail Ski Resort are all owned by the same company. Check their Web sites for special deals among the resorts, including special College Night rates.

▶ Montage Mountain

P.O. Box 3539, 1000 Montage Mountain Road, Scranton, PA 18505; (570) 969–SNOW; fax (570) 963–6621; snow report line (800) 468–7669; www.skimontage.com; montage@skimontage.com

Vertical drop: 1,000 feet
Highest summit: 2,000 feet
Skiable acres: 140
Trails: 21 (8 beginner, 6 intermediate, 7 advanced)
Longest run: 1.2 miles
Lift capacity: 8,000 per hour
Chairlifts: 6 (1 quad, 3 triples, 1 double, 1 tow bar)
Night skiing: Yes
Snow tubing park: Yes
Terrain park: Yes
NASTAR racing: Yes
Hours from D.C.: 3 to 4 hours
Directions from D.C.: Take I–83 north to I–81 north. Take exit 51, Montage Mountain Road, and follow the signs.

▶ Mystic Mountain

P.O. Box 188, Route 40 East, Farmington, PA 15437; (800) 422–2736; snow report line (724) 329–6982; www.nwlr.com/skiing.htm

Vertical drop: 300 feet
Skiable acres: 25
Trails: 10
Lift capacity: 2,000 per hour
Chairlifts: 2 (1 quad, 1 surface)
Night skiing: Yes
Snow tubing park: Yes
Half-pipe: Yes
Terrain park: Yes
Cross-country: Yes (8 trails)

Hours from D.C.: 3 hours

Directions from D.C.: Take I–270 north to I–70 west (Frederick, Maryland); then take I–70 west to I–68 West (Hancock, Maryland), and I–68 west to Route 40 west (exit 14). Turn left onto Route 40 west and continue for about 19 miles to Farmington. The resort is located on the right side of Route 40 west.

Notes: You can also go snowshoeing here.

▶ Ski Roundtop

925 Roundtop Road, Lewisberry, PA 17339; (717) 432–9631; fax (717) 432–2949; snow report line (717) 432–7000; www.skiroundtop.com; skiroundtop@skiroundtop.com

Vertical drop: 600 feet

Skiable acres: 100

Trails: 16

Longest run: 4,100 feet

Lift capacity: 11,000 per hour

Chairlifts: 9 (2 quads, 1 triple, 2 doubles, 2 J-bars, 1 magic carpet, 1 tubing lift)

Night skiing: Yes

Snow tubing park: Yes

Half-pipe: Yes

Terrain park: Yes

NASTAR racing: Yes

Hours from D.C.: 2 hours

Directions from D.C.: Take I–270 north to Route 15 north. At the first traffic light in Pennsylvania, turn right onto Harrisburg Street and go straight to the top of the hill. Turn right onto Old York Road, then left onto Route 177, left onto Pinetown, and left onto Roundtop Road.

Notes: Ski Liberty, Ski Roundtop, Ski Windham, and Whitetail Ski Resort are all owned by the same company. Check their Web sites for special deals among the resorts. Special College Night rates.

▶ Seven Springs

777 Waterwheel Drive, Champion, PA 15622; (800) 452–2223 or (814) 352–7777; snow report line (800) 523–7777; www.7springs.com

Vertical drop: 750 feet

Highest summit: 2,994 feet

Annual snowfall: 105 inches

Skiable acres: 275

Trails: 17

Longest run: 1.25 miles

Lift capacity: 22,200 per hour

Chairlifts: 14 (1 high-speed six-passenger, 3 quads, 5 triples, 2 rope tows, 1 handle tow, 2 magic carpets)
Night skiing: Yes
Snow tubing park: Yes
Half-pipe: Yes
Terrain park: Yes
NASTAR racing: Yes
Hours from D.C.: 3.5 hours
Directions from D.C.: Take the Beltway to I–270 north, to I–70 north, to I–76 (the Pennsylvania Turnpike) west. Get off at exit 10 (Somerset), turning right off the exit ramp at the second light; at the third traffic light, turn right onto Route 31 west. Continue for approximately 7 miles, turn left at Pioneer Park, and follow this road for about 4 miles, turning right at the first stop sign. Seven Springs will be 5 miles ahead on your left.

▶ Shawnee Mountain

P.O. Box 339, Hollow Road, Shawnee-on-Delaware, PA 18356; (570) 421–7231; fax (570) 421–4795; snow report line (800) 233–4218; www.shawneemt.com; ski@shawneemt.com

Vertical drop: 700 feet
Annual snowfall: 50 inches
Skiable acres: 125
Trails: 23 (7 beginner, 10 intermediate, 6 advanced)
Longest run: 5,100 feet
Lift capacity: 12,600 per hour
Chairlifts: 9 (1 quad, 1 triple, 7 doubles)
Night skiing: Yes
Snow tubing park: Yes
Half-pipe: Yes
Terrain park: Yes
NASTAR racing: Yes
Hours from D.C.: 5 hours
Directions from D.C.: Take I–83 to Harrisburg, then I–81 north to I–78 east, to Route 22 east past Allentown. Turn onto Route 33 north and take this to I–80 east, to Pennsylvania exit 52 (Route 209 north); from here, follow Shawnee Mountain signs.

▶ Whitetail

13805 Blairs Valley Road, Mercersburg, PA 17236; (717) 328–9400; fax (717) 328–5529; www.skiwhitetail.com; skiwhitetail@skiwhitetail.com

Vertical drop: 935 feet
Skiable acres: 108

Trails: 17 (6 beginner, 7 intermediate, 4 expert)

Longest run: 1 mile

Lift capacity: 11,200 per hour

Chairlifts: 6 (1 high-speed quad, 3 quads, 1 double, 1 surface)

Night skiing: Yes

Snow tubing park: Yes

Half-pipe: Yes, largest in region

Terrain park: Yes

Hours from D.C.: 1.5 hours

Directions from D.C.: Take I–270 north to I–70 west, exit 18. Turn right off the exit ramp. Go through the traffic light in Clear Spring, Maryland. Follow the snowflake and Whitetail signs 7 miles to the slopes.

Notes: Ski Liberty, Ski Roundtop, Ski Windham, and Whitetail Ski Resort are all owned by the same company. Check their Web sites for special deals among the resorts. Special College Night rates.

▶ Ski Windham

P.O. Box 459, Windham, NY 12496; (800) 754–9463; fax (518) 734–5732; snow report line (800) 729–4766; www.skiwindham.com; info@skiwindham.com

Vertical drop: 1,600 feet

Trails: 36 (10 beginner, 13 intermediate, 13 expert)

Longest run: 1.5 miles

Lift capacity: 11,800 per hour

Chairlifts: 7 (1 quad, 4 triples, 1 double, 1 pony lift)

Night skiing: Yes

Snow tubing park: Yes

Half-pipe: Yes

Terrain park: Yes

NASTAR racing: Yes

Hours from D.C.: 6 hours

Directions from D.C.: Located in the northern Catskill Mountains. From most areas, you'll take the New York State Thruway to exit 21. Then take Route 23 west directly to Windham.

Notes: Live Web cam. While this New York State resort is not with driving distance for weekend skiing, Ski Liberty, Ski Roundtop, Ski Windham, and Whitetail Ski Resort are all owned by the same company. Check their Web sites for special deals among the resorts.

17 Professional Sports

YOU MAY HAVE NOTICED that *Outdoor Escapes* does not include team sports such as soccer or softball leagues. It's just too hard to cover. There are probably thousands of team sports in the area—from T-ball for preschoolers to women's over-thirty soccer teams. You don't need a book to tell you how to find them—they're everywhere.

Professional sports and major-league sports teams are another matter. It's not a matter of your age or skill level; all you need to be a fan is interest. And anyone who has gone to the stadiums will tell you that watching a game in person is much different from seeing one on TV. Not a fan of watching baseball on TV? Go see a game in person; it'll change your whole perspective. It's an experience—the peanuts, the hot dogs, and getting to see everything the cameras never show. Professional sports are fun for all—albeit expensive. Go check out a game, even if it's an inexpensive minor-league game. You might be surprised.

Major League Baseball

▶ *The Washington . . . Expos?*

www.mlb.com

Ever since the Washington Senators (1924 World Series champions) left town back in 1972 to become the Texas Rangers, Washingtonians have been a little bitter about Major League Baseball. Why no franchise in Washington? It's a fair question considering that Washington has enough money and fans to support *two* major-league teams. Without pointing fingers—*Baltimore*—there are other nearby professional teams that would lose their fan base if Washington had its own team.

Expos—Expos—who's got the Expos? At the time of this printing, Washington, northern Virginia, and Portland were all trying to acquire the Montreal Expos. Best hunch says northern Virginia, but it's pretty easy to see that the Washington metropolitan area is the leader. So . . . will they be called the Senators again? Expos or Senators, you can get the game schedule, player info, and directions to the stadium from Major League Baseball's Web site.

▶ Baltimore Orioles

Oriole Park at Camden Yards, 333 West Camden Street, Baltimore, MD 21201; (410) 685–9800; orioles.mlb.com

No more Ripkens, no more Brady, no more Eddie, no more Palmiero, no more Mussina . . . sad to see all the great ones go. I'm just glad B. J. Surhoff is back.

To get there: Take I–95 north to exit 53 (I–395), or take exit 52 (Russell Street). You can also take the Baltimore-Washington Parkway north to exit 52 (Russell Street). Park at Camden Yards or one of the many parking lots downtown.

Minor League Baseball (Divisions A and AA)

Minor-league teams are a lot of fun for the whole family—and not nearly as expensive as the MLB games. Go see the stars before they get to the big show.

▶ Minor League Baseball

www.minorleaguebaseball.com

Maryland

▶ Bowie Baysox

Prince George's Stadium, P.O. Box 1661, Bowie, MD 20717; (301) 805–6000; www.baysox.com

Division AA; plays for the Baltimore Orioles, Eastern League.

▶ Frederick Keys

Harry Grove, P.O. Box 3169, Frederick, MD 21701; (301) 662-0013; www.frederickkeys.com

Division A; plays for the Baltimore Orioles, Carolina League.

▶ The Hagerstown Suns

Municipal Stadium, 274 East Memorial Boulevard, P.O. Box 230, Hagerstown, MD 21741; (301) 791–6266; www.hagerstownsuns.com

Division A; plays for the San Francisco Giants, South Atlantic League.

Virginia

▶ Potomac Cannons—formerly the Prince William Cannons

G. Richard Pfitzner Stadium, 7 County Complex Court, Woodbridge, VA 22192; (703) 590–2311; www.potomaccannons.com

Division A; formerly of the St. Louis Cardinals, now plays for the Cincinnati Reds, Carolina League.

NFL Football

▶ The Washington Redskins at FedEx Field

Lanham, MD; stadium phone (301) 276–6000; www.redskins.com

The Redskins have a beautiful new complex—one of the best facilities in the NFL and also the most expensive tickets in the league. Redskins Park is on a 200-acre site and is the largest outdoor stadium in the NFL.

Even the opposition has fun at FedEx Field. It's too bad their team didn't win.

To get there: Take I–495/I–95 north to exit 15A, to Harry S. Truman north, then turn right onto Lottsford Road and continue to Arena Drive. Or take I–495/I–95 exit 17A, turn right onto Lottsford Road, and continue to Arena Drive.

If you're traveling via the Metro, take the Orange line to either the Cheverly or Landover station, or the Blue line to the Addison Road station. From any of these stations, you can take a shuttle bus directly to FedEx Field. Buses go back and forth about every fifteen minutes. Buses start three hours before game time and end one hour afterward. A round trip will cost about $5.00, but this price may change at any time.

PGA Golf

▶ *Booz Allen Open (formerly the Kemper Insurance Open)*

10000 Oaklyn Drive, Potomac, MD 20854; (301) 469–3737; fax (301) 469–3741; www.pgatour.com

The Professional Golfers Association (PGA) Tour stops at Avenel in Potomac, Maryland annually in June. This private membership club has a beautiful and demanding par-seventy-one course—one of the best Tournament Players Club (TPC) courses in the country. Go and follow your favorite golfer—or find a nice putting green with good view lines and watch the professionals move through the course—or do a little of both.

Triple Crown Horse Racing

▶ *The Preakness Stakes*

Pimlico Race Course, Attn: Preakness Tickets, Hayward and Winner Avenues, Baltimore, MD 21215; reservations (410) 542–9400, ext. 4484 or (800) 638–3811; fax (410) 664–6645; www.marylandracing.com

One of the stops on the Triple Crown (the biggest prize in horse racing) is in our own backyard up in Baltimore. The Preakness Stakes is run at the Pimlico Race Course in mid-May. Concourse seating is outdoors but under cover and limited. Call to reserve a seat. The infield is cheaper, and it's also easier to get a ticket. Clubhouse and grandstand tickets also available; the grandstand is standing room only. Pimlico has a total capacity of about 98,000. After the finish, watch them paint the colors of the winner's silks onto a horse-shaped weather vane atop the Old Clubhouse cupola.

To get there: Take I–95 north to I–695 west to exit 18 and head east to Lochearn (Liberty Road). Go left onto Northern Parkway (seventh light), then right onto Park Heights Avenue and left onto Hayward Avenue. It's about an hour's drive from D.C.

▶ Charles Town Races and Slots

Route 340, Charles Town, WV; (304) 795–7001; www.ctownraces.com

Live thoroughbred racing Wednesday through Saturday year-round except Christmas.

▶ Colonial Downs

10515 Colonial Downs Parkway, New Kent, VA; (804) 966–7223; www.colonialdowns.com

Live thoroughbred racing and live harness racing. Call for details.

▶ Laurel Park

(301) 725–0400 or (410) 792–7775; www.preakness.com/laurel

Live thoroughbred racing. Call for details. The park is found on Route 198 (exit 33, Laurel), 4 miles east of I–95.

▶ Ocean Downs

10218 Racetrack Road, Berlin, MD; (410) 641–0600; www.oceandowns.com

Live harness racing. Call for details.

▶ Rosecroft Raceway

6336 Rosecroft Drive, Fort Washington, MD; (301) 567–4000 or (410) 792–9217; www.rosecroft.com

Live harness racing. Call for details.

▶ Timonium/Maryland State Fair

2130 York Road, Timonium MD; (410) 252–0200; www.bcpl.net/~mdstfair

Live thoroughbred racing at the end of August only. Call for details.

MLS and WUSA Soccer

Maybe you remember going to see Pele (the Black Pearl) back in the 1970s when he played against the Washington Diplomats down at RFK. The North American Soccer League (NASL) lasted from 1968 until about 1981, when it started to collapse. But the new Major League Soccer is back in Washington with D.C. United—winning three championships in the first four years of the league. The new Women's United Soccer Association has brought a new team to D.C. as well: The Washington Freedom features players like Mia Hamm and Amanda Cromwell, both Virginia locals. Both the Washington Freedom and D.C. United make RFK Stadium their home.

▶ Major League Soccer (MLS)

D.C. United, D.C. United Front Office, 14120 Newbrook Drive, Suite 170, Chantilly, VA 20151; (703) 478–6600; www.dcunite.com

▶ Women's United Soccer Association (WUSA)

Washington Freedom, Robert F. Kennedy Memorial Stadium, 2400 East Capitol Street, SE, Washington, DC 20003-1749; tickets (202) 547–3137; office (202) 547–8351; fax (202) 547–0176; www.washingtonfreedom.com

▶ RFK Stadium (Robert F. Kennedy Memorial Stadium)

DC Sports & Entertainment Commission, 2400 East Capitol Street, SE, Washington, DC 20003; (202) 547–9077; www.rfkstadium.com

Built in 1961, RFK Stadium was once the home of the Washington Redskins and the Washington Senators. Its capacity is 56,500.

To get there: The stadium is found at the corner of Independence Avenue and 22nd Street in southeast D.C. Follow Constitution East past the Capitol to Maryland Avenue. Turn left onto Maryland and go two blocks to Stanton Square. At Stanton Square, turn right onto Massachusetts Avenue. Take Massachusetts to Lincoln Park (at 12th Street). Go around Lincoln Park to East Capitol Street and turn right onto East Capitol. Follow East Capitol to the stadium.

ATP Tennis

▶ East Potomac Tennis Center

1090 Ohio Drive, SW, Hains Point, Washington, DC; (202) 554–5962; www.guestservices.com

The Wild Card Challenge is held here every June as a qualifier for the Legg-Mason Tennis Classic. Indoor and outdoor courts, seasonal membership or walk-in court rental, tennis lessons, and racquet stringing are also available.

▶ Rock Creek Park Tennis Center

William H. G. Fitzgerald Tennis Stadium, 16th and Kennedy Streets, NW, Washington, DC 20011; (202) 722–5949; fax (202) 722–5198; www.guestservices.com/rcp/; www.leggmasontennisclassic.com or www.atptennis.com

The Legg-Mason Tennis Classic is held here every July. The center includes indoor and outdoor courts, the tennis stadium, and free parking. The facility is adjacent to the Carter Barron Amphitheatre—they share the same parking lot.

18 The Arts

SO YOU WANT to get yourself some culture . . . not every outdoor escape is about running around as fast as you can. Sit down and relax. Maybe you want to watch a movie under the stars, see a Shakespeare play, listen to a little Mozart or Gershwin, read a book, or check out a few sculptures. Washington is the place to do it all.

Theater

Comedies, tragedies, musicals, and opera can all be experienced outdoors here in the Washington, D.C., area. You enjoy the same experience as those who attended the Greek amphitheaters in ancient times or the Globe Theater during the time of Shakespeare. Add a picnic to round out your afternoon outside or evening under the stars. As always, check your local weather report—umbrellas for rain, water and sunscreen for hot days, and warm clothes or blankets for a cool evening.

▶ Fort Dupont Park

Randle Circle, SE, Washington, DC; (202) 426–7723; www.nps.gov/fodu

A heavily wooded park with numerous trails running through its 376 acres, Fort Dupont was built in 1861 to guard against Confederate attacks—one of the sixty-four forts surrounding Washington during the Civil War. Summer theater is offered June through August, Friday and Saturday 7:30 to 11:30 P.M.

▶ Kennedy Center Millennium Stage

The Millennium Stage, John F. Kennedy Center for the Performing Arts, New Hampshire Avenue and F Street, NW, Washington, DC; (202) 416–8340; www.kennedy-center.org/ programs/millennium/

The John F. Kennedy Center for the Performing Arts has long put on the Millennium Stage as part of the Performing Arts for Everyone Initiative. Its goal is to stage at least one free performance every day of the year—and the center has been kind enough to bring it all to a mobile stage outdoors. Musicians from around the world—and some pretty big-name acts—have been featured through the years.

All this took place on the U.S. Capitol Lawn. Unfortunately, the Capitol Lawn is now another of the many outdoor venues affected by security concerns after 9/11. We can only hope the Kennedy Center decides upon a new permanent location for these concerts soon. Everyone has greatly enjoyed the arts outdoors.

▶ The Shakespeare Free for All

Carter Barron Amphitheatre, Rock Creek Park, 16th Street and Colorado Avenue, NW, Washington, DC; concert line (202) 426–1063; park information (202) 282–1063; www.nps.gov/rocr/cbarron.htm

The Shakespeare Theatre, 450 7th Street, NW, Washington, DC; (202) 547–1122; www.shakespearedc.org or www.shakespearetheatre.org

Now playing more than ten years, the Shakespeare Free for All has become a tradition in Washington. For about two weeks at the beginning of June, the Shakespeare Theatre puts on a play of exceptional quality in beautiful Rock Creek Park's outdoor stage, the Carter Barron Amphitheatre. The Shakespeare Theatre usually puts on a comedy, but occasionally stages a drama such as the 2001 production of *King Lear*. While the play is amazing, it's almost as interesting to watch the audience. People will show up in everything from beach clothes to tuxedos. Be comfortable. Bring along a picnic to eat before the show.

Gates open at 5:30 P.M., seating begins about 7:10 P.M., and the performance starts at 7:30 P.M. Admission is free, but tickets are required. Call the Shakespeare Theatre for ticket information. For other scheduled performances, call the National Park Service at (202) 619–7222.

▶ Wolf Trap—America's National Park for the Performing Arts

1624 Trap Road, Vienna, VA 22182; Wolf Trap information (703) 255–1900; tickets (703) 218–6500; membership (703) 255–1940; www.wolftrap.org

Wolf Trap has a season full of concerts, theater, and even opera. Pick up a schedule and check out a show. Lawn tickets are significantly cheaper than reserved seats.

To get there: Take I–66 to the Dulles Toll Road (Route 267 west), getting off at the Wolf Trap exit.

Concert Venues

There are a number of major outdoor concert venues around our area where you can see the hottest new bands.

Washington, D.C.

▶ RFK Stadium (Robert F. Kennedy Memorial Stadium)

DC Sports & Entertainment Commission, 2400 East Capitol Street, SE, Washington, DC 20003; (202) 547–9077; fax (202) 547–7460; www.rfkstadium.com

Built in 1961, RFK Stadium used to be the home of the Washington Redskins football team and the Washington Senators baseball team. With 56,000-plus seating capacity, RFK is still home to the D.C. United and Washington Freedom soccer teams and holds some major concerts.

To get there: The stadium is located on the corner of Independence Avenue and 22nd Street in southeast Washington, D.C. Follow Constitution east past the Capitol to Maryland Avenue. Turn left onto Maryland and go two blocks to Stanton Square. At Stanton Square, turn right onto Massachusetts Avenue. Take Massachusetts to Lincoln Park (at 12th Street). Go around Lincoln Park to East Capitol Street and turn right onto East Capitol. Follow East Capitol to the stadium.

▶ The Fort Reno Concert Series

Fort Reno Park, northwest Washington, D.C.; www.fortreno.com

Kids need a place to rock! Fort Reno is that place. I won't lie; this isn't RFK, and it isn't Wolf Trap. It's just an outdoor park in the middle of the city. But what's unique is that the Fort Reno Concert Series has provided free outdoor summer concerts for more than thirty-five years. Traditionally, it's a showcase for young, upcoming acts as well as established local groups. Shows are every Monday and Thursday, weather permitting. They begin promptly at 7:15, end at 9:30, and are free.

If ever there were a grassroots effort for the joy of new music, Fort Reno is it. Past participants have included Fugazi, Bob Mould, and The Dismemberment Plan. And these concerts are entirely volunteer-run at all levels. The people who help set up and clean up are described as "beautiful angels from heaven who help make Fort Reno possible." No disagreement here. If you like the shows—help out. If you don't have time, buy a T-shirt (after the show) or drop them a donation. The Northwest Youth Alliance, which puts on the concert series, desperately needs your help if the Fort Reno summer concerts are to continue. Even if you only send in $5.00, you'll be making a difference. Of course, larger donations are welcome. Donations are tax deductible. See the Web site for the latest information on where to send your contribution.

To get there: From downtown D.C., go north on Connecticut, then take a left onto Tilden after the zoo and Cleveland Park. Veer right onto Reno Road, and left onto Chesapeake.

▶ Fort Dupont Park Concerts

Randle Circle, SE, Washington, DC; (202) 426–7723; www.nps.gov/fodu

Fort Dupont offers concerts as well as theater; see the description under "Theater," earlier in this chapter.

Maryland

▶ Merriweather Post Pavilion

10475 Little Patuxent Parkway, Columbia, MD 21044; www.mppconcerts.com

www.ticketmaster.com, (800) 551–7328; in D.C. (202) 432–7328; in Virginia (703) 573–7328; in Maryland (410) 481–7328

To get there: Take the Beltway (I–495) to I–95 north toward Baltimore (approximately 18 miles), then take Route 32 toward Columbia to Route 29 north. Turn onto Broken Land Parkway (exit 18B) and take the first right into the Merriweather parking lot.

Virginia

▶ Nissan Pavilion at Stoneridge

7800 Cellar Door Drive, Bristow, VA 20136; information (703) 754–6400

www.ticketmaster.com, (800) 551–7328; in D.C. (202) 432–7328; in Virginia (703) 573–7328; in Maryland (410) 481–7328

Clear views of the stage and giant video screens make this a great concert location. Lawn tickets are significantly cheaper than reserved seats. Special low-profile lawn chairs are available for rent. A barrier-free facility, Nissan Pavilion offers assistive listening devices as well as large-print and Braille menus. Interpreters are available upon request. This is one of the largest outdoor venues around. No lawn chairs, food, beverages (other than sealed plastic containers of bottled water), or video or audio recorders. The parking lot gates usually open two hours prior to showtime, and the doors to the facility usually open an hour and a half prior. All concerts are performed rain or shine.

To get there: Take I–66 west to exit 44 (234 bypass). Continue to the second light and turn right onto Wellington Road. Nissan Pavilion is 3 miles ahead on your left.

▶ Wolf Trap—America's National Park for the Performing Arts

1624 Trap Road, Vienna, VA 22182; information (703) 255–1900; tickets
(703) 218–6500; membership (703) 255–1940; www.wolftrap.org

Lawn tickets are significantly cheaper than reserved seats.

To get there: Take I–66 to the Dulles Toll Road (Route 267 west), getting off at
the Wolf Trap exit.

The National Symphony Orchestra

The National Symphony Orchestra is based at the Kennedy Center. It plays around
the world but offers a number of outdoor shows in the area, including the West Lawn
of the Capitol, the Carter Barron Amphitheatre, and Wolf Trap. For more information, visit www.kennedy-center.org/nso/.

▶ Memorial Day Concert

This concert takes place on Sunday of the Memorial Day weekend, on the West
Lawn of the U.S. Capitol. It starts between 7:30 and 8:00 P.M. Free—no tickets required.

▶ July 4 Concert

Patriotic works are performed as a prelude to the national fireworks display. This
event is usually very crowded—arrive early. Check out the dress rehearsal for the
show on July 3 if you want to avoid the crowds and still have some fun. West Lawn,
U.S. Capitol, starting between 7:30 and 8:00 P.M. Free—no tickets required.

▶ Labor Day Concert

Held on Sunday of the Labor Day weekend, starting between 7:30 and 8:00 P.M.
West Lawn, U.S. Capitol. Free—no tickets required.

▶ Carter Barron Amphitheatre, Rock Creek Park

16th Street and Colorado Avenue, NW, Washington, DC; concert line (202) 426–1063;
park information (202) 282–1063; www.nps.gov/rocr/cbarron.htm

Usually free—call for details.

▶ Wolf Trap

For details, see "Concert Venues," above.

Carillons

Carillons are very large musical instruments. A carillonneur (player) uses wooden levers and pedals of the clavier to play their recitals. Washington, D.C., has more carillons than any other city in the United States. The concerts don't often attract large numbers, but there are some very loyal followers. Once you hear the music, you'll understand why.

▶ The Basilica of the National Shrine of the Immaculate Conception

400 Michigan Avenue, NE, Washington, DC 20017-1566; (202) 526–8300; www.nationalshrine.com

The Shrine of the Immaculate Conception in northeast D.C. is home to a fifty-six-bell carillon housed in the campanile. "Mary's Garden" is a beautiful outdoor setting where you can rest or pray while enjoying the carillon. The shrine has thirteen Sunday-afternoon concerts of carillon and organ. As with all carillons in the area, a number of distinguished guest carillonneurs play the recitals. Call for more information on recital times.

▶ The Kibby Carillon at the National Cathedral

Washington National Cathedral, Massachusetts and Wisconsin Avenues, NW, Washington, DC 20016-5098; (202) 537–6200; www.cathedral.org

This fifty-three-bell carillon is the third heaviest in the world and located in the cathedral's central tower. You can enjoy the "Bishop's Garden" while listening to the carillon bells. Another beautiful environment well suited to rest, prayer, or contemplation. Recitals take place on Saturday from 12:30 to 1:15 P.M.

▶ The National Zoo Carillon

National Zoological Park, 3001 Connecticut Avenue, NW, Washington, DC; (202) 673–4717; natzoo.si.edu

The National Zoo has a thirty-five-bell carillon located near the visitor center. The carillon has an automated system that sometimes doesn't work, but the manual operation does, so carillonneurs come in to play. There is some very beautiful artwork of animals on the carillon. From May through September 15, the zoo grounds are open daily 6:00 A.M. to 8:00 P.M.; from September 16 through April, hours are 6:00 A.M. to 6:00 P.M. Closed December 25.

▶ The Netherlands Carillon

www.nps.gov/gwmp/carillon.htm

The Netherlands gave this carillon in thanks for the aid given by the United States to the Dutch people during World War II. The gift symbolizes the friendship

The Netherlands Carillon is a fifty-bell instrument that makes beautiful music outdoors.

between the Dutch and American people, rooted in freedom, justice, and democracy. The dedication simply reads:

SO MANY VOICES IN OUR TROUBLED WORLD ARE STILL UNHEARD. FROM THE PEOPLE OF THE NETHERLANDS TO THE PEOPLE OF THE UNITED STATES.

This carillon isn't just an interesting sculpture or building nestled between Arlington National Cemetery and the U.S. Marine Corps War Memorial. The entire building is an instrument—a fifty-bell carillon. The tower has a playing cabin where the carillonneur sits. The Netherlands Carillon has an international program with guest carillonneurs from around the world.

With one of the best views of Washington available anywhere—you can see the Lincoln Memorial, Washington Monument, and Capitol lined up in a row—it's no wonder many people come to the evening concerts and bring a picnic. Outside the official concert schedule, the carillonneurs will sometimes practice during the noon hour so as not to disturb any proceedings at Arlington National Cemetery next door. During concerts, visitors are welcome to go up in the tower to watch the carillonneur perform and view the city of Washington as well as the north end of Arlington National Cemetery. Please be careful with small children.

Carillon concerts are presented May through September, on Saturday and national holidays 2:00 to 4:00 P.M. From June through August, concerts take place 6:00 to 8:00 P.M. Free; no tickets required.

To get there: The Netherlands Carillon is accessible from the Key Bridge. Take Fort Myer Drive. Continue on Meade Street and turn left onto Marshall Drive. From Theodore Roosevelt Bridge, take Route 50 west to Fort Myer Drive. Continue on Meade Street, and turn left onto Marshall Drive.

Movies

Movies outdoors are a treat. Take a picnic dinner for the kids or a date and enjoy a summer evening under the stars. You can even see a falling star or two if you're lucky. Outdoor movies are becoming more popular, especially with young families—they're fun and cheap. More townships are adding outdoor movies to their calendar of events; check your local community outreach programs for more information.

▶ Silent Films at Wolf Trap

1624 Trap Road, Vienna, VA 22182; Wolf Trap information (703) 255–1900; tickets (703) 218–6500; membership (703) 255–1940; www.wolftrap.org

Wolf Trap occasionally screens classic silent films with musical accompaniment by the National Symphony Orchestra or some other group. It's a unique experience—

you feel as though you've gone back in time to see what people experienced before the "talkies." Around the turn of the century (the twentieth century, that is), there was usually only a piano player as accompanist—my grandfather had that job—but the NSO makes a decent substitute. Lawn tickets are significantly cheaper than reserved seats.

To get there: Take I–66 to the Dulles Toll Road (Route 267 west), getting off at the Wolf Trap exit.

▶ Screen on the Green

Washington Monument, National Mall, between Constitution and Independence Avenues, SW, Washington, DC; (877) 262–5866 or (202) 619–7222

Screen on the Green is a wonderful gift by HBO and its parent company, AOL, to several large cities around the country. It brings the experience of the old drive-ins (minus the cars) to the National Mall. Movies are shown on a large screen (drive-in sized) next to the Washington Monument on Monday night for about six weeks, starting in late June or early July and continuing into the beginning of August. No movies are R rated, so you can bring along the kids. They always have a wide range of films, including adventure, romance, musicals, sci-fi, and even Hitchcock films. Movies are screened even in the rain, but will be canceled if there's a bad lightning storm. Bring a blanket or a chair. Free. Movies start at dusk.

Drive-In Movies

The classic drive-in movie theaters are American icons, but they're disappearing fast. The old Super 29 out on Route 29 in Fairfax, Virginia, is now home to a Costco and a shopping mall. The old Fredericksburg (Virginia) Drive-In was open into the 1990s but is now gone.

There are still one or two around, though, and they're still fun places for a date or a cheap movie for the family. You're outdoors, under the stars, your kids can move around and not cause a disturbance as in other movie theaters, and you're enjoying a movie—what could be better? Ironically, they hold the same attraction as they did fifty years ago. I encourage everyone to go out to the drive-in before they are all gone.

For a listing of all drive-ins still in operation, visit www.driveintheater.com.

▶ Family Drive-In Theatre

US 11 South, Stephens City, VA 22655; (540) 665–6982

Down I–66 past Manassas. This drive-in is probably the closest to D.C.

▶ *Moonlite Theatre*

17555 Lee Highway, Abingdon, VA 24210; (540) 628–7881

▶ *Bel Air Drive-In Theatre*

3035 Churchville Road, Churchville, MD 21028; (410) 734–7788

▶ *Bengies Drive-In*

3417 Eastern Boulevard, Baltimore, MD 21220; (410) 687–5627; directions (410) 686–4698

Shows start at twilight; the season ends in late October.

Literature

▶ *The National Book Festival*

East Lawn of Capitol and the Thomas Jefferson Building, 1st Street and Independence Avenue, SE, Washington, D.C.; www.loc.gov/bookfest

There are book fairs all around, usually put on by local libraries. Not too many are outdoors, for a very obvious reason—rain. But the National Book Festival, sponsored by the Library of Congress and hosted by the first lady, is an exception. The National Book Fair takes place at the Library of Congress and the adjacent grounds of the U.S. Capitol. People of all ages are invited to experience the joys of reading as more than fifty award-winning American writers engage in storytelling and readings. Pavilions for History and Current Events, Mystery and Suspense, Fiction and Imagination, Children and Young Adults, and even Storytelling are set up along with musical performances in one of the best-organized events open to the public. There are book signings, literacy program and library information, and lots of fun activities for children. It all happens the weekend after Labor Day. Take the Metro to Capitol South and walk one block north.

Artwork and Sculpture

Outdoor artwork is beautiful, intriguing, and available for all. Our city features outdoor artwork ranging from statues of fallen generals to modern art—and there's a lot of it. Look around; you may be surprised what you find.

Washington's famous monuments have some amazing sculptures at their heart, and most people know where they're located. (See chapter 19, "Places to Play," if you

The Awakening at Hains Point makes adults feel very small.

don't, and have a look at the "Downtown Washington/National Mall" map, too.) Check out the Korean War Memorial at night for the best effect. One of the newest memorials, the FDR Memorial, is fascinating. Arlington, Virginia, and Bethesda, Maryland, both have a lot of outdoor sculpture in their public spaces. Here are a few other places to see some good sculpture.

▶ West Potomac Park/Awakening Statue

Hains Point, Washington, DC

Kids love it, and it makes the rest of us feel very small. Open daily.

▶ The National Gallery of Art Sculpture Garden Ice Rink

7th Street and Constitution Avenue, NW, Washington, DC; (202) 289–3360 or (202) 289–3361; www.guestservices.com

The Sculpture Garden and Ice Rink is one of the newest and most beautiful parks in Washington. The centerpiece fountain is converted into an ice rink during the winter (see chapter 14, "Ice-Skating"). It's located within a block of the Hirshhorn Museum and Sculpture Garden.

▶ Hirshhorn Museum and Sculpture Garden

7th Street and Independence Avenue, SW, Washington, DC; (202) 357–2700; TTY (202) 357–1729; www.si.edu

Nineteenth- and twentieth-century sculptures. You'll find an outdoor sculpture garden across the street from the museum (on the Mall) as well as sculptures around the base of the building. It's located just one block over from the National Gallery of Art Sculpture Garden.

▶ Ladew Topiary Gardens

3535 Jarrettsville Pike, Monkton, MD 21111; (410) 557–9570; www.ladewgardens.com

Topiary is sculpture, but it's a living sculpture instead of the inanimate kind we're used to seeing. Have you ever seen swans floating along the waves of a yew bush? Or green hounds chasing a leafy fox? They're all sculpted out of plants at the Ladew Gardens. These are serious topiaries, which have taken years of training to perfect. This ain't no Chia Pet! Make sure you check out the giant Buddha. There are fifteen thematic "garden rooms." Self-guided garden tours over 1.5 miles of trails and twenty-two acres are available. There's also an annual plant sale, and the My Lady's Manor Steeplechase (see chapter 7, "Equestrian Activities") is held in spring for the benefit of the gardens. You'll find a cafe, too. Ladew is open from mid-April through the end of October, Monday through Friday 10:00 A.M. to 4:00 P.M., Saturday and Sunday 10:30 A.M. to 5:00 P.M.

To get there: Take the Baltimore Beltway (I–695) toward Towson to exit 27B (north). Go north on Route 146 (Dulaney Valley Road). After the Loch Raven Reservoir Bridge, bear left onto Jarrettsville Pike (Route 146). Ladew Gardens is located on your right, 5 miles north of the stoplight in Jacksonville on Route 146.

Purchasing Art

If you're looking to purchase art, check out the Eastern Market in southeast Washington or the Smithsonian Folk Life Festival down on the Mall.

▶ Eastern Market

7th and C Streets, SE, Washington, DC; (202) 546–2698; www.easternmarket.net

Located on Capitol Hill, Eastern Market is the last brick city market in the District of Columbia. The historic market building is home to performers and artists who display their talent and crafts throughout the week. On Saturday and Sunday there are craft and flea markets where vendors sell handmade wares as well as antiques and collectibles. Fresh produce and meats can be bought year-round. The market is open

Tuesday through Saturday 7:00 A.M. to 6:00 P.M., Sunday 9:00 A.M. to 4:00 P.M.; closed Monday.

▶ The Smithsonian Folk Life Festival

National Mall, between Constitution and Independence Avenues, SW, Washington, DC; www.folklife.si.edu

This unique festival celebrates the customs and cultures of different countries and various parts of the United States. Usually one or two foreign countries are featured, as well as at least two states or unique regions of the United States. The festival is free to the public, but there is a shop where you can purchase arts and crafts from the featured state or country. It operates in late June and early July, but is closed during the Fourth of July celebration.

19 Places to Play

WHETHER WE'RE RESTLESS SOULS who can't contain the urge to get out and play, or more contemplative types, sometimes all of us just want a chance to enjoy the beauty that nature holds. This chapter offers a sampling of the D.C. area's outdoor highlights—a kind of grab bag of attractions and destinations that aren't always easily categorizable. Most can be seen by car or are easily accessible for those with disabilities. Many are described more thoroughly in other chapters, and I'll direct you to where you can read about them in full. Enjoy.

Washington, D.C.

▶ Chesapeake and Ohio (C&O) Canal & Towpath

C&O Canal Visitor Center, 1057 Thomas Jefferson Street, NW, Washington, DC 20007; (202) 653–5190; www.nps.gov/choh or www.candocanal.org

Great Falls Tavern Visitor Center in Great Falls Park, Maryland, 11710 MacArthur Boulevard, Potomac, MD 20854; (301) 767–3714 or (301) 299–3613

The Chesapeake and Ohio (C&O) Canal runs 184.5 miles from Georgetown to Cumberland, Maryland. See chapter 1, "Trails," for a complete description and the "Chesapeake & Ohio Canal Towpath" map for the canal route.

▶ Carter Barron Amphitheatre

Rock Creek Park, 16th Street and Colorado Avenue, NW, Washington, DC; concert line (202) 426–1063; park information (202) 282–1063

National Park Service, National Capital Region; (202) 619–7222; www.nps.gov/rocr/cbarron.htm or www.shakespearetheatre.org

Now playing for more than ten years, the Shakespeare Free for All has become a tradition at the outdoor stage of Carter Barron, located in the beautiful Rock Creek Park. See chapter 18, "The Arts," for details.

▶ Dumbarton Oaks

1703 32nd Street, NW, Washington, DC; (202) 338–8278; www.doaks.org

Ten acres of beautiful formal gardens surround this historic nineteenth-century mansion located in upper Georgetown. Open daily, April through October.

▶ Eastern Market

7th and C Streets, SE, Washington, DC; (202) 546–2698; www.easternmarket.net

The last brick city market in D.C., this Capitol Hill favorite is filled with all kinds of fresh produce as well as arts and crafts. A flea market is held on Saturday and Sunday. The market is open Tuesday through Saturday 7:00 A.M. to 6:00 P.M., Sunday 9:00 A.M. to 4:00 P.M. Closed Monday. Also see "Purchasing Art" in chapter 18, "The Arts."

▶ The Ellipse

The Ellipse is the oval-shaped park found between the White House and the Washington Monument. It's home to many demonstrations, the National Christmas Tree (in December), the Great Menorah, and many softball games in summertime. Not as easily accessible in the wake of 9/11.

▶ Fort Dupont Park

Randle Circle, SE, Washington, DC; (202) 426–7723; www.nps.gov/fodu

Fort Dupont offers nature activities and summer theater; see chapters 1, "Trails," 5, "Biking," and 18, "The Arts," for more.

▶ Francis Scott Key Park

34th and M Streets, NW, Washington, DC

This tiny park is found just on the D.C. side of the Key Bridge in Georgetown. There's a great view of the Potomac as well as a walkway and bike path down to the C&O Canal. It's especially beautiful in spring with large patches of blooming tulips. The park has a bronze bust of Key and a beautiful flag to remind you of the Star Spangled Banner.

▶ Franklin Delano Roosevelt Memorial

West Potomac Park near Lincoln Memorial, Ohio Drive, Washington, DC;
(202) 426–6841; www.nps.gov

This is one of the newer outdoor memorials downtown—and one of the most thought provoking. Interestingly laid out with waterfalls and other galleries, the monument brings you back to the time of FDR. It borders the Tidal Basin, so it's a great place to see the cherry blossoms in spring. Open 8:00 A.M. to midnight.

▶ Friendship Arch

Chinatown at Seventh and H Streets, Washington, DC

The Arch is the gateway into Chinatown. There are 7,000 pieces of tile and golden carved dragon panels centering a marble panel with Chinese characters. Sadly, Chinatown was largely torn down to make way for the MCI arena, and many other businesses have moved as the neighborhood changed. Still, the Arch is a great place to see the dragons running through the streets during the Chinese New Year Parade.

▶ Kenilworth Aquatic Gardens

1900 Anacostia Drive, SE, Washington, DC; (202) 426–6905; www.nps.gov/nace/keaq

Guided tours are available through this twelve-acre sanctuary of water lilies and lotuses. You can see many frogs, toads, fish, and turtles in addition to all the flowering aquatic plants. Nature paths take you around the ponds. Walks and tours are available free of charge. Follow signs from Kenilworth Avenue (I–295).

▶ Korean War Veterans Memorial

Daniel French Drive and Independence Avenue, SW, Washington, DC; (202) 619–7222; www.nps.gov

The Korean War Memorial is especially moving when viewed at night. The nineteen soldiers are mirrored in the wall; the number 38 represents the 38th parallel, where the Korean War was fought. The photo-quality etchings in the granite wall are amazing. Along the walkway and at the base are the names of the Allied forces that fought as well as a Pool of Remembrance that honors all those who were killed, captured, wounded, or remain missing in action. The memorial is located to the right of the Reflecting Pool if you're looking down from the Lincoln Memorial. It's open 8:00 A.M. to midnight.

▶ Lincoln Memorial

23rd Street between Constitution and Independence Avenues, NW, Washington, DC;
(202) 426–6841; www.nps.gov

Known as the memorial that stirs the heart, the Lincoln Memorial marks the end of the National Mall. Inside is the famous statue of Lincoln, sitting in the chair and thoughtfully facing the Reflecting Pool. No, you can't sit on his lap. To the sides are some engraved readings of the Gettysburg Address and his second inaugural address. There's a gift shop inside. Open daily.

▶ Lincoln Park

East Capitol Street and Massachusetts Avenue, NE, between 11th and 13th Streets, Washington, DC; (202) 690–5155

Located in Capitol Hill. One end of the park has a statue of Mary McLeod Bethune, founder of the National Council of Negro Women and Bethune-Cookman College. At the other end of the park is the Emancipation Statue, which has Abraham Lincoln reaching out to an unshackled slave. Open dawn to dusk.

▶ National Zoological Park ("the Zoo")

3001 Connecticut Avenue, NW, Washington, DC; (202) 673–4800; natzoo.si.edu

Lions and tigers and bears—*oh my!* If you're going to the zoo, you're going to see the animals. And you'll see lots. But there are also plenty of trails here, so it's a good place for walking or an early-morning run (before all the buildings open), or to visit with the kids. The National Zoo is now the home of two pandas, Mei Xiang and Tian Tian, as well as a baby elephant, Kandula. Panda feedings take place at 11:00 A.M. and 3:00 P.M. Seal and sea lion training and elephant animal care sessions are at 11:30 A.M. most days. Don't forget to look up to see the "Orangutan Transportation System" overhead—a highway of sorts where orangutans can swing from one building to another on overhead cables. They're too high to jump down, and too strong to ever fall.

The National Zoo is free. Parking is fee based (calculated by the hour) and very limited. Lots are often filled by 9:30 A.M. during summer months. Try taking the Metro Red line to the Woodley Park/Zoo (a seven-minute walk uphill) or Cleveland Park (level walk) stop. Take the Cleveland Park stop to get there, and the Woodley Park/Zoo stop to get back—it'll be easier on you. The Zoo is open May through September 15, daily 6:00 A.M. to 8:00 P.M.; September 16 through April, daily 6:00 A.M. to 6:00 P.M. Closed December 25.

▶ National Mall

Between Constitution and Independence Avenues, SW, Washington, DC; www.nps.gov/nama

The Mall extends approximately 2 miles from the U.S. Capitol to the Lincoln Memorial. Enjoy views of the monuments and Smithsonian buildings. Open daily. See the "Downtown Washington/National Mall" map.

Visit the National Zoo to watch the panda feedings or arrive before-hours for an early-morning run.

▶ Rock Creek Park

Rock Creek Nature Center, 5200 Glover Road, NW, Washington, DC; (202) 895–6070; www.nps.gov/rocr

This 1,754-acre national park is set in a beautiful valley that's very different from the rest of Washington. See the "Rock Creek Park" map and chapter 1, "Trails," for more information.

▶ The National Gallery of Art Sculpture Garden Ice Rink

National Mall at Constitution Avenue and 7th Street, NW, across from the National Archives; (202) 289–3360 or (202) 289–3361; www.guestservices.com

The National Gallery offers this beautiful sculpture garden and skating rink. To read more about it, see chapters 14, "Ice-Skating," and 18, "The Arts."

▶ Thomas Jefferson Memorial

15th Street, SW, on the Tidal Basin, Washington, DC; (202) 426–6841; www.nps.gov

Known as the thought-provoking memorial in Washington, the famous dome-shaped rotunda stands next to the Tidal Basin. It's a site of quiet serenity while adjacent to busy highways and streets. Inside stands alone a 19-foot bronze statue of

Jefferson. Probably the destination of choice for Washingtonians in spring when it's surrounded by the cherry groves in full bloom. Open daily 8:00 A.M. to midnight.

▶ U.S. Capitol

East end of the Mall, Washington, DC; tour information (202) 225–6827

Home of the House and Senate, the Capitol of our fair nation is surrounded by beautiful little parks. You can stand on the west terrace overlooking the National Mall and one of the most amazing cityscapes in the world.

▶ U.S. National Arboretum

24th and R Streets, NE, Washington, DC; (202) 245–2726; www.usna.usda.gov

Bordered by the Anacostia River, the arboretum is an amazing forested park with 446 acres and 9.5 miles of winding roadways. See chapter 1, "Trails," for more information.

▶ U.S. Navy Memorial and Naval Heritage Center

701 Pennsylvania Avenue, NW, Washington, DC; (202) 737–2308; www.lonesailor.org

This place shows a great movie inside, but what's most amazing is the memorial outside with the masts, flags flapping in the wind, and waterfalls. A statue of a lone sailor overlooks the seas of the world; military concerts are held during spring and summer. It's open Monday through Saturday 9:30 A.M. to 5:00 P.M.

▶ Vietnam Veterans Memorial

Constitution Avenue and Henry Bacon Drive, NW, Washington, DC; (202) 634–1568; www.nps.gov

To the left of the Reflecting Pool looking down from the Lincoln Memorial, the Vietnam Memorial is open twenty-four hours a day; park rangers are on site 8:00 A.M. to midnight. The names of all 58,209 persons missing or killed in Vietnam are listed on the walls. Please be quiet and respectful when walking the path along the black granite walls. There are books at each end with names and the years of service in Vietnam so you can easily find the names of loved ones. The bronze statue of three soldiers by Frederick Hart is just at the end toward the Lincoln Memorial.

▶ Vietnam Women's Memorial

21st Street and Constitution Avenue, Washington, DC; (202) 426–6841; www.nps.gov

Just a few yards down from the sculpture at the Vietnam Memorial, this bronze statue of nurses tending a wounded soldier is dedicated to all the women who served in the Vietnam War.

▶ Washington Monument

Constitution Avenue and 15th Street, SW, Washington, DC; (202) 426–6841; www.nps.gov

It's a mighty big obelisk. This tallest of all masonry structures in the world just recently got a face-lift so you can see what it looked like (grime-free) back in 1885. Designed by Robert Mills, the monument is 555 feet, 5.1 inches tall. There are great views of D.C. from the top, as well as little pictures with descriptions so you know which building is which. Gives you a whole different view of Washington. Open in summer daily 8:00 A.M. to midnight, in winter 9:00 A.M. to 5:00 P.M.

▶ West Potomac Park/Awakening Statue

Hains Point, Washington, DC

Kids love it, and it makes the rest of us feel very small. Open daily.

Maryland

▶ Assateague

Assateague State Park, 7307 Stephen Decatur Highway, Berlin, MD 21811; (410) 641–2120; reservations (888) 432–CAMP (2267); Assateague Island National Seashore information (410) 641–1441; www.dnr.state.md.us/publiclands/eastern/assateague.html

Assateague Island on the Delmarva Peninsula is home to the Chincoteague ponies. See chapter 7, "Equestrian Activities," for a complete description of how to see (and even buy!) one of these famous horses.

▶ Catoctin Mountain Park

6602 Foxville Road, Thurmont, MD 21788-1598; (301) 271–4432

You'll feel the fall fireworks are a little brighter here during the peak leaf change. Many different trails accommodate hikers ranging from beginners to the more advanced. Scenic drives and overlooks offer panoramic views of the woods and Hunting Creek Lake. You can also camp, picnic, cross-country ski, horseback ride, swim, sail, and fish at the park. Cunningham Falls (technically part of Cunningham Falls State Park) is right across the road and fun to climb. The falls are an easy walk from the visitor center parking lot.

To get there: From the Beltway, take I–270 north to I–70 north to Route 15 north. Take a left onto Route 77 and follow the signs to the visitor center to pick up a *Guide and Map to the Park*. It's about a ninety-minute drive from Washington, D.C.

▶ Great Falls Park

Great Falls Tavern Visitor Center, 11710 MacArthur Boulevard, Potomac, MD 20854; (301) 767–3714 or (301) 299–3613; www.nps.gov/choh or www.candocanal.org

Everyone knows Great Falls, but most visitors to the area can't believe such spectacular falls can exist so close to Washington. There is an amazing visitor center here, and you can even ride on the *Canal Clipper*—a mule-drawn canal boat whose crew members, dressed in 1870s style, tell the story of the canal. The park is right along the C&O Canal, and offers many other "billy goat" trails. There's some climbing here, but better rock is available on the Virginia side. Other than the *Canal Clipper,* the entire park is wheelchair accessible. Though there are ramps even on the bridges to Olmstead Island, much of the area is rough gravel and not the easiest to get around on. If you are mobile but have a hard time getting around, you can get a wheelchair on loan at the tourist center. Also see chapter 4, "Climbing."

▶ Ladew Topiary Gardens

3535 Jarrettsville Pike, Monkton, MD 21111; (410) 557–9570; www.ladewgardens.com

Flower gardens and topiary gardens. Yes, it's north of Baltimore and an hour and a half away—but if you have the chance to visit these gardens, you'll understand why they're a must-see. See chapters 1, "Trails," and chapter 18, "The Arts."

You don't have to be a child to enjoy *The Fox Chase* at Ladew Topiary Gardens in Monkton, Maryland.

▶ Patuxent Research Refuge

National Wildlife Visitor Center, 10901 Scarlet Tanager Loop; Laurel, MD 20708; (301) 497–5760

Nature hikes and tram tours of the woods. Live hawks, owls, and reptiles, plus exhibits. Admission is free.

Maryland/Virginia

▶ White's Ferry

24801 White's Ferry Road, Dickerson, MD 20842; (301) 349–5200

The only regularly operating ferry on the Potomac River, historic White's Ferry has been working the upper Potomac for the last 170 years. See chapter 8, "Boating."

Virginia

▶ Arlington National Cemetery

Across Memorial Bridge from Lincoln Memorial, Arlington, VA; www.mdw.army.mil or www.arlingtoncemetery.org

You can partake in a self-guided walking tour or a shuttle tour of the Arlington National Cemetery; information is available at the visitor center. The national burial ground is 600 acres largely of white gravestones. Some of the more prominent graves are those of President John F. Kennedy, Supreme Court Justice Thurgood Marshall, and world-champion boxer Joe Louis. Come see the renowned Changing of the Guard at the Tomb of the Unknown Soldier. Free admission.

Arlington is open daily 8:00 A.M. to 5:00 P.M.; from April through September, it's open until 7:00 P.M. Also see chapter 7, "Equestrian Activities," (to read about the cemetery's horses), and chapter 18, "The Arts" (on its carillon).

▶ Chincoteague National Wildlife Refuge

Refuge Manager, Chincoteague National Wildlife Refuge, Chincoteague, VA 23336; (757) 336–6122; chinco.fws.gov

The Virginia side of Assateague Island (lower part) has biking and hiking trails, beaches, marshes, waterfowl, and the famed Chincoteague ponies. See chapter 1, "Trails," and chapter 7, "Equestrian Activities," for more information.

▶ George Washington's Mount Vernon Estate and Gardens

George Washington Parkway (south end), Mount Vernon, VA 22121; (800) 429–1520; www.mountvernon.org

The estate is on 500 acres overlooking the Potomac River; it's located 16 miles from Washington and 8 miles from historic Old Town Alexandria. Open daily. In March, September, and October, the hours are 9:00 A.M. to 5:00 P.M.; April through August, it's open 8:00 A.M. to 5:00 P.M.; and from November through February, you may visit from 9:00 A.M. to 4:00 P.M.

▶ Great Falls National Park

9200 Old Dominion Drive, Great Falls, VA 22066; (703) 285–2965; www.nps.gov/gwmp/grfa/

The Potomac cut through Mather Gorge to create these famous falls, which are beautiful at any time of year. Occasionally you'll see kayakers running the falls; almost always you'll see kayakers surfing the rapids below the falls. Climbers enjoy the cliffs on both sides of the Potomac. (See chapter 4, "Climbing.") There are trails along the clifftops, and horses ride through the park as well. Picnic areas. The park closes at dusk; the visitor center is open daily 10:00 A.M. to 5:00 P.M. Admission is $4.00 for noncommercial vehicles.

▶ The Netherlands Carillon

www.nps.gov/gwmp/carillon.htm

The Netherlands gave the Carillon in thanks for the aid given by the United States to the Dutch people during World War II. Chapter 18, "The Arts," tells the full story of this stunning gift.

▶ Potomac Overlook Regional Park

Northern VA Regional Park Authority, 2845 North Marcy Road, Arlington, VA; (703) 528–5406; www.nvrpa.org/potomacoverlook.html

Nature center, nature trails, hikes, and concerts are all on offer at this park located at the end of Marcy Road, off Military Road in North Arlington. It's open all year during daylight hours.

▶ Riverbend Park

8700 Potomac Hills Street, Great Falls, VA; (703) 759–9018

Nature Center, 8814 Jeffery Road; (703) 759–3211

This relatively unknown park encompasses 400 acres of forest, meadows, ponds, and streams bordering the Potomac. The gates are open 7:00 A.M. to dusk; hours are posted. The gate is locked at closing time. There are also picnic tables and a boat ramp for private launches. You can rent canoes here. It's located just up the Georgetown Parkway from Great Falls. Turn onto River Bend Road; the park is at the end.

▶ Skyline Drive, Shenandoah National Park

(540) 999–3500; www.nps.gov/shen/

Skyline Drive at Shenandoah National Park is one of the most popular places to visit to see the fall colors. Skyline Drive is 105 miles long and boasts about seventy scenic overlooks. The park itself has 500 miles of trails, including the Appalachian Trail, and is only 75 miles west of Washington, D.C. It's accessible by I–66 and Route 340 (to the north entrance at Front Royal), Route 211 (for the central entrance at Thornton Gap), Route 33 (at Swift Run Gap), and I–64 (at the Rockfish Gap entrance). Skyline Drive is the only road through Shenandoah National Park. Entrance fees. Call or check the Web site for current fees and information.

▶ Theodore Roosevelt Island

(703) 289–2550; www.nps.gov/gwmp/tri.htm

Theodore Roosevelt Island's ninety-one wooded acres sit out in the middle of the Potomac River across from the Kennedy Center. See the "Theodore Roosevelt Island" map and chapter 1, "Trails," for a description.

20 Playdates

TRYING TO PLAN your next outing? Aunt Gertrude's boys are coming to town next month but you have no idea where to take them? Have to plan your "summer" vacation in March but not sure which week to take? You know about fun activities in July but what about January, when the winter blues have got you down? We've all been in need of a calendar full of fun things to do. This is that calendar. Special events happen year-round in our nation's capital. Here are some of the best; check individual chapters for more events centered on your particular interests.

Winter

▶ Chinese New Year

Sometime between January 21 and February 19; (202) 357–2700

Gung Hay Fat Choy! Celebrate the Chinese New Year down in Chinatown, see the Friendship Arch, and watch the Chinese New Year Parade. The Chinese welcome in the New Year by chasing away evil spirits. Watch the huge cloth dragon and the lion dancers as well as the marching bands in the parade, which begins at 5th and H Streets.

January

▶ Presidential Inauguration Day

January 20

Not quite an annual event, Inauguration Day is still a constant for Washington. Presidential inaugurations are the American answer to royalty celebrations; some say

A sea of people at the Capitol watch as the president is sworn in on Inauguration Day.

they are our coronations. Despite the uncertainty of political life in Washington, we are guaranteed a big inaugural celebration once every four years. The week preceding the inauguration has become a spectacle in itself as the people are whipped into a frenzy for that fateful day. The Mall becomes a tent city with bands playing on stages and various cultural events to celebrate our democracy. The people-watching is amazing. When else do you get to see Native American congressmen riding horses through the streets of D.C. in their native costumes?

The day itself is January 20. One of the Supreme Court justices always administers the oath of office after the election as decreed by the Twentieth Amendment (the Lame Duck Amendment) in 1933. It's hard to get close to the terrace on the West Front of the Capitol to see the actual swearing-in. The grounds are barricaded, and you need a ticket to get in. Take binoculars whether you have a ticket or not. Tickets are given to senators and representatives, who in turn give them to their constituents. Call your congressman to get a ticket. Do it early, not the week before the inauguration. If you can't get a ticket, find some friends in a faraway state and see if they can get a ticket for you. Lying and cheating to get good inauguration tickets? You'll feel like a Washington insider. Don't forget the inaugural parade back to the White House after the oath when the president and first lady always make that impromptu walk among the peasants.

February

▶ Groundhog Day

February 2

At Gobbler's Knob in the small town of Punxsutawney, Pennsylvania, there lives a groundhog named Phil. Every February 2, Phil comes out of his hole after a long winter's sleep to look for his shadow. See chapter 13, "Cloud-Watching and Natural Science," for the full story of the festivities surrounding this celebrity woodchuck.

▶ Lincoln's Birthday

February 12; (202) 619–7222

There is a wreath-laying ceremony and a reading of the Gettysburg Address at the Lincoln Memorial. For more information on the Lincoln Memorial, see chapter 19, "Places to Play."

▶ Frederick Douglass's Birthday

(202) 619–7222 or (202) 426–9961; www.nps.gov/frdo

Frederick Douglass, abolitionist and adviser to President Lincoln, was born in 1817 or 1818. Like many slaves, his real birth date is unknown. The celebration of his life takes place in mid-February with a wreath-laying ceremony at the Frederick Douglass National Historic Site in Anacostia.

▶ George Washington's Birthday

February 22—but celebrated on President's Day, the third Monday of the month; (703) 838–4200 or (703) 838–5005

There is a parade down Washington Street in Old Town Alexandria as well as a number of Revolutionary War reenactments.

Spring

▶ The Annual White House Easter Egg Roll

White House; 1600 Pennsylvania Avenue, NW, Washington, DC

White House Visitor Center (corner of 15th and E Streets); (800) 717–1450, (202) 208–1631, (202) 456–2200, or (202) 456–7041; www.whitehouse.gov

This is a crazy experience on the White House Lawn in the disguise of a fun day for children. Free timed tickets are distributed, with a limit of four per person, beginning at 7:00 A.M. on the day of the roll at the visitor pavilion on the Ellipse south of the White House. The line starts really early. Parents should try not to be surly. The event is open to children eight and under with an accompanying adult. The event is usually held on the Monday after Easter. Occasionally this event is only open to men and women of the Armed Services and their families. Please call for details.

▶ The Cherry Blossoms of Washington

Late March through early April

The flowering cherry blossoms signify the end of winter for Washingtonians. We crawl out of our winter shells and migrate down to the Tidal Basin after watching the news to see which weekend will be the "peak" time. Chapter 1, "Trails," tells the full story of the famous cherry trees and where to see them.

▶ The National Cherry Blossom Festival

Late March through early April; parade information (202) 728–1135; general information (202) 547–1500

This two-week celebration of the blooming cherry trees has been in existence since 1935. Since 1954 the festival has been kicked off by the traditional Japanese Lantern Lighting ceremony at the Tidal Basin. The major event is the National Cherry Blossom Parade.

For locals, cherry blossoms signify the end of winter and are a cause for outdoor celebration—which explains the National Cherry Blossom Festival.

March

▶ St. Patrick's Day

March 17; (202) 637–2474

St. Patrick's Day brings a parade down Constitution Avenue from 7th to 17th Streets; it starts at noon. Tickets are available for grandstand seating. Floats, dancers, and bagpipers, and it's all followed by a festival of music and dance.

Old Town Alexandria also has a St. Patrick's Day parade, but it's not usually held on March 17; the date varies. For information, call (703) 838–4200.

▶ Kite Day at the National Air and Space Museum, Gunston Hall Kite Festival, and the Smithsonian Annual Kite Festival

Mid- to late March

See chapter 10, "Kite Flying," for descriptions of these three great spring festivals.

▶ Run vs. Row 10K Challenge & 4K Walk, along with the Washington DC Marathon

Late March

Chapter 3, "Running," describes these annual races.

April

▶ Thomas Jefferson's Birthday

April 13; (202) 619–7222

The celebration of our third president includes a wreath-laying ceremony at the Jefferson Memorial along with military drills. See chapter 19, "Places to Play," for more information on the Jefferson Memorial.

▶ Alexandria Garden Tour

Late April; (703) 838–4200

Private gardens and historical sites are open to the public.

May

▶ Shenandoah Apple Blossom Festival

Early May; Winchester, VA; (540) 662–3863; www.sabf.org

The festival is so big that it has *two* parades, a large number of bands, arts and crafts, bluegrass and country music concerts, and dances. Lots of fun.

▶ The Virginia Gold Cup Races

First Saturday in May

See chapter 7, "Equestrian Activities."

▶ The Preakness Stakes

Mid-May

One of the stops on the Triple Crown (the biggest prize in horse racing) is held in our own backyard up in Baltimore. See chapter 7, "Equestrian Activities," for a full description of this event.

▶ Memorial Day at Arlington National Cemetery

(202) 475–0856

Ceremonies include a wreath laying at the Kennedy grave site, a presidential wreath laying at the Tomb of the Unknown Soldier (usually the president, but sometimes another high-ranking official, will preside), and services at the Memorial Amphitheatre.

▶ Memorial Day at the Vietnam Veterans Memorial

The celebration includes a wreath-laying ceremony.

▶ Rolling Thunder—Ride for Freedom

Sunday of the Memorial Day weekend

The largest motorcycle rally in Washington. See chapter 6, "Motorcycle Riding," for all the details.

▶ Memorial Day Concert by the National Symphony Orchestra

Sunday of the Memorial Day weekend

See chapter 18, "The Arts," for more information on this concert and other concerts by the National Symphony Orchestra.

▶ Trinity Episcopal Church Annual Stable Tour (aka Hunt Country Stable Tour)

Memorial Day weekend

See chapter 7, "Equestrian Activities," for more information on this self-guided tour.

Summer

▶ Kennedy Center Millennium Stage

June 5 through Labor Day

See chapter 18, "The Arts," for more information on these free outdoor performances.

▶ The Netherlands Carillon Concerts

May through September

See chapter 18, "The Arts," for more information on these summer concerts.

▶ Polo on the Mall

Summer

See chapter 7, "Equestrian Activities," for more information.

▶ Great Meadows Polo

June through the first week of September

See chapter 7, "Equestrian Activities."

▶ Mule-Drawn Barges of the C&O Canal

Summer

See chapter 7, "Equestrian Activities," for more information on these rides.

▶ Middleburg Polo

Mid-June through September

See chapter 7, "Equestrian Activities," for more information on this polo club.

▶ Screen on the Green

Late June or early July through early August

See chapter 18, "The Arts," for more information on these large-screen outdoor movies.

▶ Civil War Reenactments

Summer; www.firstmanassas.com

A ring of forts surrounded Washington, D.C., during the Civil War. Maryland had its State House surrounded by federal troops, and legislators were confined to house arrest so the state could not vote to secede with Virginia and the rest of the South. Still, there are a lot of battlefields in the D.C. area.

- *Bull Run* near Manassas, Virginia, is west down I–66.
- *Fredericksburg* lies an hour's drive down I–95 south from Washington.
- *Gettysburg* is found north in Pennsylvania up I–270.
- *Locust Hill Farm* is at the intersection of the Route 15 Bypass and Route 15 north, just north of Leesburg, Virginia. The 140th anniversary of First Manassas was the largest Civil War reenactment and living history event ever held in Virginia.

June

▶ National Race for the Cure

First Saturday in June

See chapter 3, "Running," for contact and registration information.

▶ The Shakespeare Free For All

Early June

See chapter 18, "The Arts," for more information on these plays in Rock Creek Park.

▶ Booz Allen Open

Early June

The Professional Golfers Association (PGA) Tour stops at Avenel in Potomac,

Maryland, annually in June. See chapter 17, "Professional Sports," for contact information.

▶ Potomac Celtic Festival

Early June; P.O. Box 11160, Burke, VA 22009-1160; (800) 752–6118; www.potomaccelticfest.org

An enchanting celebration of Celtic traditions and cultures including pipe bands, a ceilidh, folk art, authentic foods, storytellers, and much, much more. Held at Morven Park's International Equestrian Center.

▶ Flag Day

June 14

Fly our nation's colors! A national flag was first proposed on June 14, 1777. To commemorate that, we fly our flags and celebrate our country on this date. If you would like to purchase a flag flown over the U.S. Capitol, you can do so through your local senator or representative—easily reached via www.senate.gov or www.house.gov. Order a 3- by 5-foot flag or one 5 feet by 8 feet, both made of either cotton or nylon. There is a small fee for flying, certification, shipping, and handling. Checks are made payable to "Keeper of the Stationery." An official certificate will accompany each flag. A spirited present for any patriot.

▶ The Annual Hall of Fame Joust, Natural Chimneys Regional Park

Third Saturday in June

See chapter 7, "Equestrian Activities," for information on this event and other jousting tournaments at Natural Chimneys Regional Park.

▶ The Smithsonian Folk Life Festival

Late June, early July

See chapter 18, "The Arts," for more information on this celebration of national and international cultures and customs.

▶ CCA Downriver Race

June

See chapter 8, "Boating," for more information on this race sponsored by the Canoe Cruisers Association.

▶ Old Dominion 100-Mile Ride

June

See chapter 7, "Equestrian Activities," for more on this endurance horse race.

▶ The Wild Card Challenge

June

A qualifier for the Legg-Mason Tennis Classic; see chapter 17, "Professional Sports."

July

▶ Independence Day

July 4

Fourth of July celebrations in the nation's capital include a spectacular and patriotic parade that marches past many of our historic monuments, a concert on the Capitol steps by the National Symphony Orchestra, and a fireworks display near the Washington Monument.

▶ National Symphony Orchestra July 4 Concert

See chapter 18, "The Arts," for more information on this free concert.

▶ Chincoteague Pony Crossing and Auction

Last Wednesday and Thursday in July

See chapter 7, "Equestrian Activities," for more information on this unique breed.

Get a glimpse of the unique Chincoteague ponies on Pony Swim Day and at the Pony Auction on Assateague Island.

▶ Legg-Mason Tennis Classic

July

See chapter 17, "Professional Sports," for more information on this annual event, held at the Rock Creek Park Tennis Center.

▶ Scottish Highland Games

July; Episcopal High School, 3901 West Braddock Road at Quaker Lane

Virginia Scottish Games, P.O. Box 1338, Alexandria, VA 22313; (703) 912–1943; vascottishgames.org

August

▶ The Governor's Cup Yacht Race

First weekend in August

See chapter 8, "Boating," for more on this regatta at St. Mary's College of Maryland.

▶ Natural Chimneys Jousting Tournament

Third Saturday in August

See chapter 7, "Equestrian Activities," for more on this historic tournament.

▶ Calvert County Jousting Tournament

Last Saturday in August

See chapter 7, "Equestrian Activities," for more on this tournament, including the children's competition.

▶ The National Frisbee Festival

End of August

On the National Mall near the National Air and Space Museum. Lots of disks, and the dogs are amazing.

▶ Hot Air Balloon Festival and Flying Circus Airshow

August

See chapter 9, "Aviation," for more on these two events.

▶ The Old Town Alexandria Irish Festival

August

This Irish Festival in Old Town is held down at Waterfront Park, on the riverfront between Prince and King Streets. Music, arts and crafts, other activities. Admission is free.

Autumn

▶ *Maize Maze*

Late August through October

See chapter 1, "Trails," for more information on this corn maze in Leesburg, Virginia.

▶ *Maryland Renaissance Festival*

Late August through mid-October

See chapter 7, "Equestrian Activities," for more on this medieval jousting festival.

▶ *Fall Foliage*

The fall foliage is at its peak around Washington in mid-October. Rain, temperature, and time factors determine how soon, how late, and how long the peak colors last. Great places to view the foliage include:

- U.S. National Arboretum (see chapter 1, "Trails").
- The National Mall (chapter 1, "Trails," includes a description).
- Virginia's Skyline Drive at Shenandoah National Park (see chapter 19, "Places to Play").
- Catoctin Mountain Park in Maryland (also described in chapter 19, "Places to Play").

September

▶ *Irish Festival*

Labor Day weekend; Montgomery County Fairgrounds, Gaithersburg, MD;
(301) 565–0654; www.ncta.net

Produced by the National Council for the Traditional Arts and begun in 1976, this festival has changed venues many times as it has grown larger. Even with the growth, it has still had some troubles and was canceled in 2001. Hopefully this great festival will continue on. It includes lots of performers, six concert stages, an Irish dance hall, Irish-American authors, an Irish marketplace, sheepdog herding, Irish draft horse jumping, and more.

▶ *National Symphony Orchestra Labor Day Concert*

See chapter 18, "The Arts," for more on this annual event.

▶ *The National Book Festival*

Weekend after Labor Day

See chapter 18, "The Arts," for more on this outdoor book fair, sponsored by the Library of Congress.

October

▶ AIDS Walk

Early October

See chapter 3, "Running," for more information on registering for this fund-raising event.

▶ The Army 10 Miler

Mid-October

See chapter 3, "Running," for more on the world's largest 10-mile race.

▶ The White House Fall Garden Tours

Mid-October; White House, 1600 Pennsylvania Avenue, NW, Washington, DC

White House Visitor Center (corner of 15th and E Streets); (800) 717–1450, (202) 208–1631, (202) 456–2200, or (202) 456–7041; www.whitehouse. gov

The beautiful gardens are open to the public, and you get a chance to see the famous Rose Gardens and the South Lawn.

▶ The International Gold Cup Races

Third Saturday in October

See chapter 7, "Equestrian Activities," for more information.

▶ The Marine Corps Marathon

Fourth Sunday in October

See chapter 3, "Running," for more on this open-registration marathon.

▶ Lantern Tour in Old Town Alexandria

October; Old Town Alexandria Visitor Center; (703) 548–0100

The October tour schedule is greatly expanded so we can all enjoy those things that go bump in the night. See chapter 2, "Walking," for more information on days and times.

▶ Ghost Walk to the Grave of Edgar Allan Poe

Halloween

See chapter 2, "Walking," for more on this spooky tour in Baltimore.

FOLIAGE RESOURCES

- **The National Forest Service Fall Color Hotline,** (800) 354–4595. Updated weekly.
- **Maryland Fall Foliage Hotline,** (800) 532–8371. Includes events listings.
- **West Virginia,** (800) CALL–WVA (225–5982).
- **The Weather Channel,** www. weather.com. Perhaps the best Web site for fall foliage information.
- **Weather Net 4 (NBC),** wxnet4. nbc4.com/chap1/foliage.html.
- **Virginia's Skyline Drive at Shenandoah National Park,** www.nps.gov/shen/.

November

▶ Veteran's Day

Mid-November celebration activities include services at Arlington National Cemetery, the Vietnam Veterans Memorial, and the U.S. Navy Memorial, as well as an 11:00 A.M. wreath-laying ceremony at the Tomb of the Unknown Soldier. Activities are led by the president or another high-ranking official.

▶ Jingle Bell Race

Weekend after Thanksgiving

See chapter 3, "Running," for more on this race in which runners wear tiny jingle bells on their shoelaces.

December

▶ Warrenton Christmas Parade

Early December; Main Street, Warrenton, VA; (540) 347–4414; www.historicwarrenton. org

▶ Lighting the National Christmas Tree

Second weekend in December at dusk; (202) 208–1631

On the Ellipse until January 1. The lighting is usually done by the president of the United States (sometimes from elsewhere in the country) and starts off the annual Pageant of Peace. Includes the National Christmas Tree as well as trees representing every state and territory. Musical performances every night (except December 24 and 25) from 6:00 to 8:30.

▶ Lighting the People's Christmas Tree (aka the Capitol Holiday Tree)

Mid-December; (202) 619–7222

The Speaker of the House traditionally flips the switch to light the People's Tree. Celebrations include military band performances and holiday songs. Located on the West Lawn of the U.S. Capitol.

▶ Lighting of the Great Menorah

Beginning of Hanukkah

Celebrate the beginning of the Festival of Lights at 5:00 P.M. on the northwest corner of the Ellipse near Constitution Avenue.

Where's Santa? The kids have to be in bed when he comes or he won't leave them any presents. So what could be better than tracking his progress via up-to-the-minute updates on the Internet? You can also learn all the technical specifications of Santa's sleigh, and view photos and movies. NORAD, the military installation that tracks missiles, has tracked Santa every Christmas Eve since 1958. Check out the Official NORAD Tracks Santa Clause Web Site (www.norad santa.org) and the Santa Cam. Merry Christmas.

▶ The Christmas Festival of Lights at the Mormon Temple

Early December through January 1; Church of Jesus Christ of the Latter Day Saints, 9900 Stoneybrook Drive, Kensington, MD; schedule of free nightly events (301) 587–0144

The lighting of the National Christmas Tree on the Ellipse is not what it once was. The government can only go so far in stripping the tree of any religious symbolism before it takes out the festive holiday feeling altogether . . .

Instead, *the* outdoor place to go during the Christmas season is the Mormon Temple's outdoor display. The Mormon Temple is perched high on a hill overlooking the northwestern section of the Beltway. Every tree and bush is covered with hundreds of thousands of tiny multicolored lights that make this place come alive. Not only are the grounds beautiful and festive, but there's also a Nativity scene with real people playing the parts of the holy family on the first Christmas night. Look for the display from 5:30 to 10:00 nightly.

To get there: Take exit 33 off the Beltway and turn right onto Beach Drive, then left onto Stoneybrook.

▶ First Night

New Year's Eve

There are many New Year's Eve celebrations and parties around the area, but how many are outdoors? First Night celebrations are a nice combination of open air and warming indoor spots to celebrate the birth of the New Year. Lots of local towns from Annapolis to Winchester have their own version of First Night, each with its own events—be they bands, or fireworks, or fire trucks. Most are nonalcoholic, but check first. The nonalcoholic ones are just as much fun, are family oriented, and offer a little better environment for the kids.

- Alexandria, (703) 836–1526
- Annapolis, (410) 280–0700
- Baltimore, (800) 282–6632
- Fredericksburg, (800) 678–4748 or (540) 373–1776
- Leesburg, (703) 777–6306
- Montgomery County, (301) 217–6798
- Warrenton, (540) 349–0010
- Winchester, (540) 722–6367

21 Backyard Arena

WHEN OUR MOTHERS TOLD US to "go outside and play," it wasn't merely to play. It was also to compete in serious contests of strength, agility, and skill. These weren't games; they were the sports we grew up with. The title was on the line each and every summer afternoon right after lunch. Sure, we all know the rules to kickball or Wiffle ball. They're the same as baseball except with kickball, you can bean the base runner. But there are a number of other "sports" that we sometimes forget about, or else the rules slip our minds. Compete with your friends and family in your backyard arena and pass along the traditions.

Kickball

Do you have enough people for two teams and a big red ball? Then you're ready! The rules are just like baseball, but you can bean the base runner. (Of course, you have to hit below the shoulder.) The object is to score more runs than the opposing team. It's your game—ghost players are optional based upon how many people you have—tie goes to the runner—no bouncies—and come up with some good taunts for the opposing pitcher.

▶ Kickball on the Mall

The World Adult Kickball Association (WAKA); www.worldkickball.com; info@worldkickball.com

Kickball is enjoying an amazing comeback. Adults who grew up on the sport have decided that there's really no reason to stop playing, so they've started adult leagues. The World Adult Kickball Association had it origins in Washington, D.C., as long ago as 1998. They do play with rules, so you know they're serious. No bouncies, no head-shots, one base on an overthrow, forced outs, and no ghost players. Games are played at the base of the Washington Monument starting in May and go all summer long. Several area bars and restaurants now sponsor divisions around the area, including Kelly's Irish Times (located at 14 F Street, NW, in D.C.), where players like to meet after the games. I wonder what they do there? If you're interested in playing, fill out the contact form on the Web site. In 2002 WAKA had thirteen divisions in D.C., northern Virginia, Maryland, and San Francisco, and more than 4,000 people playing. Numbers are expected to triple in 2003, and new divisions will likely pop up in other cities around the country. League kickball is a great fun social-athletic opportunity to . . . go outside and play.

Pitching Horseshoes

So you've got some horseshoes and some dirt . . . you're ready to go pitching. You'll need at least four horseshoes and two dirt or sand pits with iron stakes in the middle. The stakes should be about 40 feet apart. Players stand at a stake and take turns tossing or pitching two horseshoes at the other stake. A ringer is when the horseshoes are wrapped around the iron stake (the horseshoe hitting the iron stake will make a "ringing" sound). Ringers are three points. If no one scores a ringer, the closest shoe gets a point—but it has to be within a horseshoe width to count as a point. The first person to fifty points wins—but if you're out just to have fun, you can change your winning score to suit your time schedule.

For an official rules handbook with in-depth rules including horseshoe size and regulation height of the stake, contact the National Horseshoe Pitchers Association of America.

▶ *National Horseshoe Pitchers Association of America (NHPA)*

www.horseshoepitching.com

▶ *The Winchester Horseshoe Club*

P.O. Box 2141, Winchester, VA 22604; www.geocities.com/Colosseum/Sideline/5366/Winc/winchest.html

League play from May through September.

▶ *Frederick Horseshoe Pitchers Association (FHPA)*

P.O. Box 4027, Frederick, MD 21705; (301) 846-3483; horseshoe.htmlplanet.com

June through August at Maryvale Park on West Patrick Street, across from Frederick Middle School, in Frederick, Maryland.

Croquet

Croquet is the game where you hit the balls with a mallet through the wickets (little gates) and try to hit the stake at the end. There are two teams (with one, two, or three players each), which take turns striking the balls. Each team has to navigate its two or three balls through the wickets. The first team to get its balls through all the wickets (in the correct direction) and hit the stake wins.

In the backyard/toy version of croquet, you play with nine wickets, setting them out in whatever interesting course you like—taking into consideration the size of the lawn. Hitting your opponents' balls (called roqueting) is part of the fun. If an opponent's ball lands directly next to yours, you can step on your ball and hit it so that it drives your opponent's ball far, far away. It'll take him a few strokes to get back where he started. This was how my friends and I used to play. Granted . . . we weren't really following the rules, but we still had fun. Knock your little sister's ball into the azaleas!

The full-blown International or American Rules Croquet is a little different from the backyard version of the game. Played on huge flat greens that make golf courses envious, each team must use certain-colored balls; roqueting causes bonus strokes. It is always a double-diamond configuration, with necessary allowances for obstacles and terrain. But there's always a center wicket surrounded by four side wickets, and two wickets and a stake at either end of a course approximately 100 feet long and 50 feet wide. "Is he making a break from the baulk lines? That's just not done!" Using the complete rules makes croquet more civilized and turns it into an interesting and sometimes tense game of skill. The sport sets, designed for adults, are elegant pieces of hardware; the mallets are graceful, perfectly weighted, and designed to give you the gravity stroke essential for playing the sport seriously. The nine-wicket game is the most popular, and less intimidating than the six-wicket version. It also was the original way croquet was played. The French invented it, the Irish popularized it, and the British perfected it. Now big in the States, croquet is truly an international sport.

Golf Croquet

Golf croquet is a little different and takes only about thirty minutes to play. The rules and set paths/courses can be found on the www.CroquetAmerica.com Web site. You won't find a better explanation of the different kinds of rules and the settings in which they're played. Good for family outings on a summer day.

Advancing

So you've played for a while, enjoy the sport, and want to become an advanced player. Join a U.S. Croquet Association club, purchase some instruction tapes, or take a three-day intensive course. They're lots of fun and will help you further your skills.

Associations

The U.S. Croquet Association headquarters staff can answer any questions about membership, learning the game, organizing a club, building a lawn, or getting croquet started at an existing lawn sport facility. The offices of both the U.S. Croquet Association and the Croquet Foundation of America are now on site at the National Croquet Center in West Palm Beach, Florida.

▶ U.S. Croquet Association (USCA)/National Croquet Center/Croquet Foundation of America/Croquet World Online Magazine

700 Florida Mango Road, West Palm Beach, FL 33406; (561) 478–0760; fax (561) 686–5507; www.CroquetAmerica.com, www.croquetworld.com, or www.CroquetNational.com; USCA@msn.com

Local USCA Clubs

The following D.C.-area croquet clubs invite public inquiries:

▶ Baltimore Country Club

Baltimore, MD; (410) 889–4400

▶ Patuxent Croquet Club Inc.

Elkridge, MD; (410) 381–6234

There are two lawns at the Patuxent Club at Larriland Farms in Columbia, Maryland, about forty-five minutes from D.C. Guests are welcome. Call for directions and reservations.

▶ Underground Croquet Club

Kensington, MD; (301) 962–9722; info@sportingclassics.com

Nonclub member play is not permitted at the Underground Croquet Club.

▶ Capital City Croquet Club

Arlington, VA; (703) 549–1339

▶ Great Falls Croquet Club

Vienna, VA; (703) 759–3231

▶ Green Gazebo Mallet Club

Fairfax Station, VA; (713) 569–8495; rgillett@chickenout.com

Equipment

Mallets, wickets, and stakes . . . sounds very British, doesn't it? Most croquet sets are basically toy sets that you get at the mall for $39.95 up to $150.00 or more. The cheapest sport sets—designed for adults with the gravity stroke essential for playing the sport seriously—are about $400. Four-player sets are available from many sources, which you can review in the manufacturer directory at www.Croquet America.com.

▶ The National Croquet Calendar

P.O. Box 208, Monmouth, OR 97361-0208; (503) 838–5697; www.croquet.com/calendar

This great croquet periodical has listings of croquet equipment—products and services.

▶ *Clarkpoint Croquet Company*

P.O. Box 137, Southwest Harbor, ME 04679; 207-244-9284; www.clarkpoint.com

If you'd like to order a beautiful sport-quality croquet set, check out Clarkpoint Croquet Company. This Maine firm makes sets from domestic and exotic woods—round or square, with brass binding or not. Sets are available in bags, boxes, or stands. Individual mallets and components can be purchased separately. The sets come as a nine-wicket (American) or six-wicket (international) game. The company offers more products than those listed on its Web site, so you may want to ask for a catalog.

▶ *Croquet Sport Company*

P.O. Box 4218, Seattle, WA 98104; (206) 722–1321; www.deweyusa.com/deweyusa/croquet

Do you need standard or tournament wickets? Garden or tournament mallets, clips, stakes, or even corner pegs? Croquet Sport has anything you could need for your croquet outing—all made with fine craftsmanship.

For More Information

▶ *Croquet Web*

heracles.itsc.adfa.edu.au/~sme/croquet/croquetweb/

The best Web site for croquet links is from Australia.

▶ *The World Croquet Federation*

www.worldcroquet.u-net.com

The world authority on croquet.

▶ The World of Croquet

www.croquet.com

An excellent rules section to settle your disputes.

▶ Oxford University Croquet Club

users.ox.ac.uk/~croquet

For coaching on the lawns or varsity matches.

▶ Dublin University Croquet Club

www.maths.tcd.ie/local/JUNK/croquet/croquet.html

Just in case you're visiting New Square during the summer.

▶ Croquet Association

www.croquet.org.uk

Thanks to the U.S. Croquet Association and Clarkpoint Croquet Company for all of their assistance in providing valuable croquet information. They truly are advocates for the sport. Check out their Web sites—then go play some croquet!

Bocce and Pétanque

The Italians call it bocce and the French call it pétanque, but most people don't know one from the other. Both are fun versions of lawn bowling where strength and age factor little. Anyone can participate, and even the beginners can play with the experts.

BOCCE	PÉTANQUE
Italian origin	French origin
played on a court	played anywhere
target is the pallino	target is the wooden jack
ball is called a bocce	ball is called a boule
bocce is usually made of resin	boule is metal
bocce is rolled	boule is tossed or lobbed
12 points to win	13 points to win

Game tactics and counting of points are similar for both.

Bocce

The purpose of the game is to roll the bocce (a ball about the size of a grapefruit) as close as possible to the pallino, a 1.75-inch ball, which is rolled down the alley first. The bocce closest to the pallino scores. The first team with twelve points wins the game.

To learn the open bocce regulations of the United States Bocce Federation, visit www.bocce.com.

Pétanque

There are two teams (between one and four players per team), which toss their boules (metal balls) toward a target (wooden jack). The jack is thrown out about 10 meters. The teams take turn tossing boules to get as close to the jack as possible. The winning team gets as many points as it has boules closer to the jack than the closest boule of the losing team. The first team to get thirteen points wins.

For complete rules, see www.petanqueamerica.com.

Badminton

Just because you're hitting little "birdies" back and forth across a net with tiny light rackets, doesn't mean this game is easy. Badminton, an Olympic sport, is a lot more challenging than most people realize. It is the world's fastest racquet sport, and not only do you have to be pretty quick, but good aim is also important. The shuttlecock (birdie) can't touch the ground during a rally—it's fun to watch the players jumping, twisting, and flailing about to avoid this. Most backyard lawn sets are combination volleyball and badminton sets, so finding a set is easy.

▶ USA Badminton (USAB)

Olympic Plaza, Colorado Springs, CO 80909; (719) 578–4808; www.usabadminton.org; info@usabadminton.org

USAB is the recognized national governing body for the sport of badminton in the United States. It oversees all U.S. badminton competitions and prepares the best players for the Olympic games.

Badminton Clubs

Many nearby schools have their own badminton clubs—including the University of Maryland, St. Albans, GWU, and Howard University—but there are a few public clubs in the area.

▶ *Virginia Badminton Association*

Warren Emerson, 4306 North 39th Street, Arlington, VA 22207; (703) 534–6815

▶ *Korean American Badminton Association*

William Hong, P.O. Box 197, Annandale, VA 22003; (703) 625–6990;
fax (703) 820–7198; hancorea@yahoo.com

Tetherball

You start with a pole about 10 to 12 feet high. The tetherball (similar to a volleyball) is attached to a string or rope tied to the top of the pole. The string or rope is about 8 to 10 feet long. There are two players, one standing on each side of the pole; they try to hit the ball in opposite directions. The game is won when the string or rope is completely wrapped around the pole so it no long spins and the ball hits the pole.

Volleyball

Volleyball was begun back in the late 1800s and is a combination of basketball, tennis, baseball, and handball. Volleyball has a net about 6.5 feet high and is played on backyard lawns, beaches, indoor courts, and even in swimming pools. There are two teams with at least two people per team. The serving team hits the ball over to the receiving team, and the two teams volley back and forth until the ball hits the ground or is hit out of bounds. Other than the serve, each team has only three hits to get the ball over to the other side. You can only hit the ball—no throwing. A point is won by a team when its opponents allow the ball to hit the ground or hit the ball out of bounds. The player keeps serving until her team hits the ball out or allows the ball to hit the ground on its side of the court. Then the receiving team gets a chance to serve. All players usually have a chance to serve—they rotate, just like a batting order in baseball. There are many lawn sport sets available, and most include volleyball equipment.

You can often find many people playing volleyball down on the Mall between Constitution and Independence Avenues, SW, in D.C.

▶ *USA Volleyball*

715 South Circle Drive, Colorado Springs, CO 80910; (888) 786–5539;
www.usavolleyball.org

USA Volleyball is the national governing body for the sport of volleyball in the United States and is recognized by the Fédération International de Volleyball (FIVB) and United States Olympic Committee (USOC). You can download an official book of rules or a score sheet from the organization's Web site.

▶ Mid-Atlantic Volleyball (MAV)

13017 Wisteria Drive, #334, Germantown, MD 20874; (301) 972–3611; www.mavolleyball.org

MAV promotes volleyball activities in the Washington area. It serves players with clinics, leagues, tournaments, and equipment. The group hosts grass and sand tournaments as well as tournaments down on the National Mall.

Chess

While it's a little different from the backyard arena games we grew up with, chess can be a great way for family members to enjoy a beautiful day together out on the balcony or in the backyard. But more often there are places in cities across the country where people congregate just to play this game of kings. A board, the pieces, and an opponent are all you need. Chess began in India sometime between A.D. 500 and 700. The pieces and rules have changed a bit, but it's still a game of strategy with a rich tradition.

Fun as it is, people often have the misconception that chess is too difficult or takes too long to play. In reality, even the uninitiated can learn in a very short time, and you can always find someone on your playing level. Try a game of Blitz Chess—moves must be made within five minutes. This may seem like a lot of time, but most games only last about eight minutes with a maximum of an hour or so. As with all games, the more you play, the better you become. Check out your local library for books to help players on all levels.

Chess in the D.C. Area

In D.C. *the* place to go is Dupont Circle. While it's not quite as popular as Washington Square up in New York City, you can still find a game here almost anytime.

▶ Human Chess Match

Maryland Renaissance Festival, Crownsville, MD; (800) 296–7304; (410) 266–7304

The Maryland Renaissance Festival—a celebration of sixteenth-century life—offers a unique Human Chess Match that is played every day of the festival at the Jousting Arena. The time is listed in the program. Come join in the fun—you, too, can be a piece on the board if you arrive early enough. This is an old-style match: If one piece is to take another piece, the two people (representing the pieces on the board) go out and fight a hand-to-hand combat. I'm not certain this ever took place in history, but it sure is fun to watch. While they do get a few people from the crowd to serve as pieces, the events are well scripted and no "civilians" actually end up fighting.

The festival runs from the end of August into the middle of October; hours are Saturday and Sunday (as well as Labor Day) from 10:30 A.M. to 7:00 P.M. Call for admission prices.

To get there: The festival takes place near Annapolis in Crownsville, Maryland. Take Route 50 east to Route 3 north, drive 2 miles to Route 450 east, then go 6 miles east to Crownsville Road. Turn left and drive 0.5 mile to the festival.

▶ U.S. Chess Center

1501 M Street, NW, Washington, DC; (202) 857–4922; www.chessctr.org

The U.S. Chess Center is open Monday through Thursday 6:00 to 9:00 P.M., weekends noon to 6:00 P.M. The folks here do more than just sell good chessboards and organize tournaments. They work a lot with kids and schools, organize the Anacostia Chess League, and sponsor the Chess Kids on Saturday.

▶ U.S. Chess Federation

3054 NYS Route 9W, New Windsor, NY 12553; (800) 388–5464; www.uschess.org

The U.S. Chess Federation is the official, not-for-profit U.S. membership organization for chess players of all ages and levels. Its online shop has a large selection of books and equipment for everyone from beginners to grandmasters. Pick up a wide variety of timing clocks. To order a USCF membership, catalogs, or correspondence chess, please call the toll-free number.

For More Information

- Maryland Chess Association, www.serve.com/mdchess.
- Virginia Chess Federation, www.vachess.org.
- Chess Is Fun, www.princeton.edu/~jedwards/cif/intro.html.
- World Chess Federation, www.fideonline.com.

Cricket

You may be saying, "I never played cricket growing up!" And you may be right, but then again not everyone grew up around here. It shouldn't be surprising that the Washington, D.C., area—with its international flavor—has many cricket enthusiasts. Nor should it be surprising that it has a rather large cricket league, with more than twenty-five teams from Baltimore to Fairfax. But in order to have a game that doesn't take all day, the league teams play only thirty-five overs (or at least no more than forty). This puts the time to play somewhere between two and three hours instead of the eight to ten hours required for the traditional one-day game.

So if you're an old cricketer, find a team in your area and see if they have any room for another player. If you're not quite ready to bat some 6s or bowl leg spin, at least go watch a match. Maybe if you pick up a few of the rules, you'd get the courage to go play. At least you'd be able to talk about Yorkers and googlies like an expert.

▶ Washington Cricket League

(877) WICKETS (942–5387); www.wclinc.com

The Washington Cricket League is made up of all the cricket clubs around Virginia, Maryland, and D.C. There are currently two leagues (Lincoln and Jefferson), with three divisions (Upper, Middle, and Lower).

How to Play Cricket

Cricket is a game played between two teams. One team bats while the other fields. There is a pitcher who throws the ball in to the batter. The batter tries to make runs, while the pitcher tries to throw the batter out. The pitcher even has special pitches, such as a curveball or a slow pitch. If the batter hits the ball into the field, the fielders try to catch it to get an out, or try to get the ball back in to a certain area before the batter gets there—again, scoring an out.

So . . . it's just like baseball, right? No, not really. Maybe you've seen some pictures of cricket or some video footage of a game. First off, you notice that everyone is wearing 1920s tennis clothes. Then you see a guy running and making an awkward throw at the feet of another guy wearing huge ice hockey goalie leg pads while trying to hit the ball with some sort of long flat paddle—and there are some sort of croquet sticks in the ground behind the batter. Or at least that's the typical American impression.

The Field Setup

First off, there are eleven players on each side instead of nine. And yes, there are sticks behind the batter. These three vertical sticks are called wickets—and sometimes stumps. On top of the wickets, there are horizontal sticks called bells. The field is set up like a circle—it's a rope, usually. The bowling and batting is in the middle. Unlike baseball, the ball can be hit behind the batter—that's fine, and the ball remains in play. And this makes sense when you realize that you've got a ball coming in at a high speed, bouncing in front of the batsman, and a flat bat that can put a ball off in almost any direction.

Bowling

The goal of the bowler (pitcher) is to hit the wickets and bells. The bowler can even bounce the ball in front of the batter to make it more difficult to hit or block. The goal of the batter is to hit the ball or, at a minimum, defend the wickets. If the wickets are hit, the batsman is "bowled" or what we would call "out," and then another batsman (player) comes up to bat. The bowlers have special pitches like a "googly" (a spinning ball, much like a curveball) or a "Yorker" (which comes in and hits the wickets directly without bouncing first).

So, to recap, the bowler bowls a Yorker, the batsman misses, the ball hits the wicket, and the batsman is bowled. Got it? Great! Let's move on.

The Bowler

The bowler must use a full arm swing—which looks like a large overhead swing. The proper bowling technique is needed. If the ball is pitched like a baseball, then it's considered a "no ball" or an invalid bowl. In addition, the bowler must release the ball before crossing a line, or give up a run (similar in baseball to a walk and taking a base).

There are six pitches in each "over."

On every new over, the team must switch bowlers. A single bowler can bowl, at most, ten overs. The captain decides who bowls. If a bowler has too many "6s" (similar to home runs), then the captain will send him to the field.

The Batsman

The batsman's goal is to hit the ball and make runs. If the ball is hit up in the air and caught, the batsman is out. If the ball is hit in the air and goes over the boundary (rope), then it counts as six runs (like a home run). If the ball is hit along the ground, the fielders miss it, and it crosses the boundary, then it counts as four runs.

All in all, not too bad so far. So you're saying to yourself: *But I've seen cricket, and there are actually two sets of wickets and two guys out there with bats, so what's up with that?* Well, there *are* two batsmen. The wickets have an area on either side of them called a crease. When one batsman is batting, the other batsman stands in the opposite crease. If a ball is hit into the field but doesn't go over the boundary, the two batsmen will try to run over to the opposite crease. If the batsmen can cross each other and get into their own crease, then they score a run. And the distance isn't huge, so they can keep going and may try to cross over a second or even third time—for a second or third run.

The Fielders

(We had to get to the fielders at some point.) The fielders' main goal is to catch a ball to make the batsman out. But there is another way for fielders to get a batsman out. If the batsman hits along the ground and runs, the fielders try to throw the ball back in and knock over a wicket. The fielders usually throw the ball in to the wicket keeper (similar to a catcher in baseball). The wicket keeper will then knock down the wicket. If the fielders—including the wicket keeper—can knock down the wicket before the batsman gets to the crease, then the batsman is out.

The One-Day Game—Wickets and Overs

There is a five-day game, which we won't go into here. The one-day game is what's played professionally, played locally, and seen on television.

A toss at the beginning of the game determines who bats and who fields. This might be a good time to mention that *wicket* is also the word for an out—as if it weren't confusing enough! So what about balls and strikes? There aren't any. A single batter can keep hitting until bowled or fielded out. There are ten wickets for each team before the next team can bat. You may think there should be eleven, since there are eleven players, but remember, there must be two batsmen out there to create a run. So when the tenth batsman is out, it's time for the other team to bat.

You may also be thinking: *But the batsman doesn't have to run and could just sit there and defend the wickets all day long—how does this game ever end?* Well, that's a good point, and it plays into the strategy of the game, but the batsman can't actually sit there all day long and take the pitches. Remember how there are six pitches in an over? In the one-day game, there are only fifty overs for each team. So your goal as a batsman is to make as many runs as you can before it's time for the other team to bat. The second team at bat is only trying to make one more run than the first team.

Recap

The first team at bat has fifty overs, seven wickets (outs), and 243 runs. In this case, the team got the complete number of bowls before ten batsmen were bowled. The second team had forty-three overs, nine wickets, and 244 runs.

The second team won. While they had more batsmen bowled out, they scored more runs before they were bowled out completely or had all fifty overs. Now that you have the basics—go outside and play!

For More Information

▶ *BBC*

news.bbc.co.uk/sport/

The best Web site around for online learning, fun games, and tracking of professional cricket matches is undoubtedly the BBC's. Do a search for "Last Man Standing." The Web link will probably change over time, but the search for it on the BBC site shouldn't be hard. It's a wonderful and fun way to play cricket online. Learn as you go. Take a Yorker head-on and go for a 6!

▶ CricInfo.com

www.cricinfo.com

CricInfo.com is another British-based cricket page with features and all the news you need to follow your favorite team.

▶ U.S. Cricket

www.uscricket.com

For more information about cricket around the United States.

ABOUT THE AUTHOR

Kevin Carnahan developed a love of nature at a very early age thanks to his parents, who often told him to "go outside and play." He has lived in the Washington, D.C., area his entire life and has participated in just about every sport and activity within these pages. After years of telling friends and family about fun places to go, he decided to compile his lists and descriptions into this, his first book. Kevin received his bachelor of arts degree from Mary Washington College and works at a large Internet company by day. He lives in Arlington, Virginia.